GRADES **4–8**

Spelling
The **READING PUZZLE**

D1594917

Elaine K. McEwan
Linda M. Nielsen

CORWIN PRESS
Classroom

For information:

Corwin Press
A SAGE Company
2455 Teller Road
Thousand Oaks, California 91320
CorwinPress.com

SAGE, Ltd.
1 Oliver's Yard
55 City Road
London EC1Y 1SP
United Kingdom

SAGE India Pvt. Ltd.
B 1/I 1 Mohan Cooperative
Industrial Area
Mathura Road, New Delhi
India 110 044

SAGE Asia-Pacific Pvt. Ltd.
33 Pekin Street #02-01
Far East Square
Singapore 048763

Printed in the United States of America.

ISBN: 978-1-4129-5826-4

This book is printed on acid-free paper.

08 09 10 11 12 10 9 8 7 6 5 4 3 2 1

Executive Editor: Kathleen Hex
Managing Developmental Editor: Christine Hood
Editorial Assistant: Anne O'Dell
Developmental Writer: Linda M. Nielsen
Developmental Editor: Collene Dobelmann
Proofreader: Carrie Reiling
Art Director: Anthony D. Paular
Design Project Manager: Jeffrey Stith
Cover Designers: Michael Dubowe and Jeffrey Stith
Illustrator: Roger Audette
Design Consultant: The Development Source

Acknowledgment from Elaine McEwan: To Raymond, husband, business partner, and a fabulous speller.

Acknowledgements from Linda Nielsen: A special thanks to my good friend and colleague, Rob Edison, and to my niece, Katie Cueva, for contributing such delightful stories. Much appreciation also to my very supportive husband, Jim, whose background and knowledge as an educator provided the perfect sounding board.

GRADES **4–8**

TABLE OF CONTENTS

Introduction

Just as Gertrude Stein once said that "a rose is a rose is a rose," a spelling rule is a spelling rule. Students need systematic, direct instruction on spelling fundamentals. Internalizing spelling rules helps to free students' thought processes so they can write more effectively. This book presents the spelling rules and their exceptions in a concise, fun, and interactive way with a variety of activities and games.

It provides structured, teacher-directed spelling practice for upper elementary and middle school students. Each chapter provides a teaching strategy that limits the amount of new information students receive at one time so they can internalize one spelling skill before moving on to another.

How to Use This Book

The chapters in this book are organized by common spelling rules. Start with any chapter that contains fundamentals your students need to learn. In order to ensure that students internalize the spelling rules and new vocabulary words in each chapter, continue to review them as you explore subsequent chapters. With this method, your students will automatically remember spelling rules and correctly write vocabulary words.

Use the introductory lesson at the beginning of each chapter to present a particular spelling rule. Follow the suggestions provided in each activity regarding what to write on the board, what to say, and what student responses might be. Photocopy and give students the Spelling Rules chart provided on pages 6–7 and encourage them to use the chart as a reference. After you have completed the activities at the beginning of each chapter, use the reproducible pages and games to engage students in practicing the spelling rules. The last reproducible in each chapter is a quiz on a particular spelling rule or rules. As with any assessment, use the results to determine which students need additional help and reteaching before you move on to another chapter.

The last chapter, "Assessment," challenges students to remember all of the spelling rules covered throughout the book. Use these assessments formally or informally to determine which students need a particular rule or rules reviewed or retaught.

As students gain confidence in spelling proficiency, confidence in their writing ability will also grow. When students master the spelling rules in this book, they will be able to put more energy into their creative "what" to put on paper and not labor over "how" to spell the words. Better spellers will become more effective, willing writers.

Put It Into Practice

Unfortunately, spelling is one of those skills that can get lost in the curriculum. However, one's ability to spell is usually associated with educational attainment, accuracy, and neatness, whereas poor spelling is a sure sign of illiteracy to many (Personke & Yee, 1971).

There is a strong connection between spelling and reading skills. Researchers agree that reading and spelling are interdependent (Ehri, 1991) and that knowledge of one or the other can be of mutual benefit.

This is why spelling is one of the pieces of the Reading Puzzle essential for students to put in place as they acquire literacy skills. The Reading Puzzle is a way of organizing and understanding reading instruction, as introduced in my book, *Teach Them All to Read: Catching the Kids Who Fall Through the Cracks* (2002). The puzzle contains the essential reading skills that students need to master in order to become literate at every grade level. *The Reading Puzzle, Grades 4–8* series focuses on five of these skills: Word Analysis, Comprehension, Fluency, Vocabulary, and Spelling.

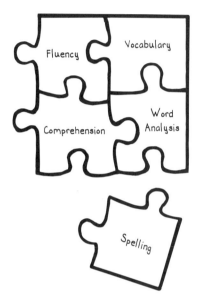

While spelling seems like a relatively straightforward skill, in reality, it encompasses a variety of skills: "the ability to recognize, recall, reproduce, or obtain orally or in written form the correct sequence of letters in words" (Graham & Miller, 1979, p. 76). Reading is a decoding process that moves from symbols to sounds, and spelling is an encoding process that maps from sounds to symbols. The connection is clear.

According to the research, successful spelling instruction should:

- Be teacher directed and include systematic practice with controlled amounts of new information

- Include multisensory elements (saying, writing, and visualizing words)

- Be organized and sequential, following a natural word order that corresponds to phonological development

- Emphasize high-frequency words that are used in writing

- Begin with phonemic strategies and move on to morphemic strategies for words made up of prefixes, suffixes, and bases

- Use the test-study-test method in which teachers first determine what students know and then expect them to learn the words they do not already know

Spelling Rules

RULES	EXAMPLES	EXCEPTIONS
CHAPTER 1: THE FIRST SPELLING RULES		
i Before e—*i* before e, except after c, or when it sounds like /ā/ as in *neighbor* and *weigh*	niece, believe; receive, ceiling	weird, seizure, foreign, seize, species, leisure, neither, either, their, height, omniscient
Using *a* and *an*—Use *an* before words beginning with a vowel or a vowel sound.	an apple, an herb garden; a violin, a university	
CHAPTER 2: SILENT LETTERS		
Silent *b*—after *m* and before *t*	lamb, thumb, debt, doubt	
Silent *g*—before *n* or *m*	sign, gnome, phlegm	
Silent *h*—usually at the beginning of a word, but also silent after a vowel at the end of a word, and after *r* or *k*	herb, honor, oh, hurrah, rhinoceros, khaki	
Silent *k*—at the beginning of a word before *n*	know, knight	
Silent *l*—usually before *m*, *f*, or *k*, and in *could*, *should*, and *would*	calf, salmon, stalk	
Silent *p*—when *p* begins a word and the second letter is *n*, *s*, or *t*	pneumonia, psychic, pteranodon	
Silent *t*—silent in words ending in -*sten* and -*stle*	glisten, castle	
Silent *w*—at the beginning of a word before *r*, and a few other words	write, wreath, answer, sword	
CHAPTER 3: CONTRACTIONS		
1. Keep all of the first word. (TIP: The words *there are* cannot be combined to form a contraction.)	can't, haven't, hasn't	See Rule #3.
2. Place the apostrophe where the letter or letters are missing.		
3. There is one exception! *will not = won't* Note: *It's* is always a contraction meaning *it is. Its* with no apostrophe shows singular possession.	*Its* feet were muddy after the rain. *It's* raining today.	
CHAPTER 4: PLURAL NOUNS		
Add *s* in most cases.	student/students	Listen for the /f/ sound in a plural noun (e.g, graphs, chiefs, gulfs, beliefs, roofs, puffs).
Add *es* to words ending in *s*, *sh*, *ch*, *x*, and *z*.	bus/buses; wish/wishes; speech/speeches; fax/faxes; quiz/quizzes	
Change *f* or *fe* to *v*, and add *es*.	elf/elves; wife/wives	

RULES	EXAMPLES	EXCEPTIONS
Change y to i when a consonant comes before the y, and add es.	country/countries	
Keep the y and add s when a vowel comes before y.	monkey/monkeys	
Add es to words ending with a consonant and o. Add s if a vowel precedes the o.	tomato/tomatoes radio/radios	Add s to musical terms. (piano/pianos; cello/cellos) Some o words form plurals with s or es. (zeros/zeroes)
In hyphenated compound words, add s to the base noun.	sister-in-law/sisters-in-law	
Some nouns have irregular plural forms.	child/children	
Some nouns have the same spelling in both singular and plural forms.	deer/deer; sheep/sheep	

CHAPTER 5: PREFIXES

RULES	EXAMPLES	EXCEPTIONS
When adding prefixes, the spelling of the base word does not change.	preview, semiannual	
Sometimes a hyphen separates the prefix and the base word.	anti-inflammatory	
Use a hyphen before a capital letter.	post-Victorian, pre-Columbian	

CHAPTER 6: SUFFIXES

RULES	EXAMPLES	EXCEPTIONS
Final e—Drop the final e when the suffix begins with a vowel. Keep the final e when the suffix begins with a consonant. Keep the final e when it is preceded by a vowel in the base word.	make + ing = making hope + ful = hopeful see + ing = seeing	like/likeable; knowledge/knowledgeable
Doubling—Double the last consonant when a one-syllable word ends with CVC (consonant-vowel-consonant) and the suffix begins with a V (vowel). Extension: Also true when a multisyllabic word ends with CVC (i.e., cur, gin, mit, pel) and the suffix begins with a V.	stop + ed = stopped recur + ed = recurred; permit + ing = permitting; compel + ed = compelled	
Ending y—Change y to i when a word ends in a consonant and y, and the suffix is anything but -ing. Keep the y when a word ends in a vowel and y, and the suffix is -ing.	happy + ness = happiness; study + ing = studying	
Add k—When words end with c, add k before suffixes that begin with e, i, or y.	panic + ed = panicked; garlic + y = garlicky	
en—When a word ends with w, add the suffix -en, and drop the e.	blow + en = blown; know + en = known	
al—When a word ends with ic, add al before adding the suffix -ly.	basic + al + ly = basically; medic + al + ly = medically	public/publicly
ion/or—Use the or spelling on the end of a noun if a form of the word ends in ion (meaning state, quality, or act). If not, use the er ending (meaning one, who, or that which).	profession/professor; direction/director	If not, use the er ending. (teach/teacher; build/builder)

CHAPTER 7: HOMOPHONES

RULES	EXAMPLES	EXCEPTIONS
Homophones sound the same but have different meanings and spellings.	close/clothes; there/their/they're	

CHAPTER 1

The First Spelling Rules

Students easily memorize the *i*-before-*e* rule, but the exceptions to this rule often leave them confused about when to apply it. It's best to teach the rule directly and then teach the few exceptions. Have students memorize these words.

Rule

i before e, except after c, or when it sounds like /ā/ as in neighbor and weigh

i Before *e*

1. Write on the board several words that have an *ei* spelling after the letter *c* (e.g., *receive, deceive, perceive, conceive, ceiling*). Underline the *ei* spelling in each word and say with students: ***i* before *e*, except after *c*.**

2. Write the symbol for long *a* on the board: /ā/. Review the long *a* sound. Ask students to think of words that have a long *a* sound and an *ei* spelling (e.g., *neighbor, weigh, eight, vein, veil, sleigh, eighty, eighteen, reign*). Write the words on the board. Underline the *ei* spelling to emphasize the rule and the spelling pattern. Say with students: ***i* before *e*, except after *c*, or when it sounds like /ā/ as in *neighbor* and *weigh*.**

3. Write exceptions to the rule on the board. Have student groups create mnemonic phrases or acronyms to help them remember the exceptions to the *i*-before-*e* rule. Exceptions to the rule include: *weird, seize, species, leisure, neither, either, their, height, caffeine, protein, omniscient.* For example: *Weird omniscient species seize either their protein or caffiene for leisure.*

4. Create a Word Wall. List regular *ie* words, *ei* letter combinations that come after *c*, *ei* words that have a long *a* sound, and exceptions to the *ei* rule.

5. Using the Spelling Bee Word List, have student groups compete to see who can correctly spell the most words.

Spelling Bee Word List

seize	species	weighed	patient	freight
friend	neighbor	receive	reviewed	chief
height	veins	sleigh	reins	leisure
niece	reindeer	eighty	shrieks	piece
neither	veil	believe	weird	
either	reign	their	deceive	

Name _____ Date _____

Do You Know *ie*?

Directions: Unscramble each word and write it on the line.

Rule
i before *e*, except after *c*, or when it sounds like /ā/ as in *neighbor* and *weigh*

1. rrdineee _____

2. getfirh _____

3. sinve _____   **4.** eneic _____

5. zeeis _____   **6.** ridwe _____

7. yethig _____   **8.** efdrni _____

9. lieveeb _____   **10.** grinbeho _____

Directions: Write *yes* if the word follows the *i*-before-*e* rule. Write *no* if it does not.

11. seize _____   **12.** receive _____

13. friend _____   **14.** their _____

15. veil _____   **16.** species _____

17. veins _____   **18.** niece _____

19. reign _____   **20.** deceive _____

21. either _____   **22.** height _____

23. reindeer _____   **24.** believe _____

25. freight _____   **26.** leisure _____

27. neither _____   **28.** sleigh _____

29. chief _____   **30.** weird _____

Name _____ Date _____

i-Before-e Practice

Directions: Circle the word that is spelled correctly.

(recieve, receive)   (niece, neice)   (believed, beleived)

(patient, pateint)   (relieved, relieved)   (shrieks, shreiks)   (decieving, deceiving)

(piece, peice)   (chief, cheif)   (frieght, freight)   (riegn, reign)

(riendeer, reindeer)   (friend, freind)   (sliegh, sleigh)   (reviewed, reveiwed)

(wieghed, weighed)   (ieghty, eighty)   (riens, reins)   (nieghbor, neighbor)

Directions: Use each word above only once to fill in the blanks in the story.

Win a Race or Friends?

Last week, my [1]_____ who lives in Alaska was practicing with her dogs for the Iditarod race on the frozen icy tundra. As she held the [2]_____ in her hands and yelled, "Mush," she noticed a large herd of [3]_____ in the valley below. She [4]_____ there were probably [5]_____ animals altogether. When evening came, a cold winter wind began blowing across her face. She quickly guided her [6]_____ across the wilderness to a familiar village. The [7]_____ of the village had been her [8]_____ for as long as she could remember. His [9]_____ as chief had now lasted thirty-five years. Everyone was glad to see her. [10]_____ of happiness and welcome filled the air. The smell of roasting meat made her stomach growl. She hoped to make a deal by delivering some of the villagers' heavy [11]_____ to the city, and in return [12]_____ a [13]_____ of meat for herself and each of her dogs. But she had to be [14]_____ while the villagers discussed her offer. They finally agreed.

In the morning, she began her trek across the barren countryside back to the city. The heavy packages from the village had been [15]_____, and she realized they [16]_____ many more pounds than she had thought. Her dogs strained with each step. She was proud and [17]_____ as they pulled the load the last mile into the city. Back at home in her own bed, she [18]_____ the events of the past week. Overall, it had been a good practice run. Her dogs were stronger, and she had helped her long-time [19]_____.

Do You Know *ie* Better!

Directions: Read each sentence. Circle each correctly spelled word in parentheses.

1. My (nieghbor's, neighbor's) dog howled all night at the moon.

2. The frown on my mom's face led me to (believe, beleive) that she was not pleased.

3. Blood is carried back to the heart through our (viens, veins).

4. In order to have a balanced meal, we had to decide between (iether, either) broccoli or spinach for our vegetable.

5. The tallest basketball player's (hieght, height) was 7'4".

6. My sister's daughter is my (niece, neice).

7. The teacher's stern appearance was very (decieving, deceiving) because underneath he had a very kind heart.

8. Matthew (reviewed, reveiwed) his geography notes carefully every night the week before the test.

9. Humans belong to a different (species, speceis) than other animals.

10. Snails must have a lot of (patience, pateince) because they move so slowly.

Directions: Write *ie* or *ei* on the lines to correctly spell each word.

11. n _____ _____ gh

12. b _____ _____ ge

13. f _____ _____ ld

14. v _____ _____ l

15. l _____ _____ sure

16. p _____ _____ ce

17. t _____ _____

18. th _____ _____ r

19. th _____ _____ f

20. p _____ _____ r

21. gr _____ _____ f

22. p _____ _____

i-Before-*e* Quiz

Directions: Circle each correctly spelled word in parentheses.

> **Rule**
> *i* before *e*, except after *c*, or when it sounds like /ā/ as in *neighbor* and *weigh*

Waiting for Santa

For [1](eighteen, ieghteen) minutes the [2](reindeer, riendeer) had waited. They were [3](queit, quiet) and [4](pateint, patient), and [5](their, thier) hair ruffled in the wind. The [6](freight, frieght) for the flight was already loaded onto the [7](sleigh, sliegh). But [8](neither, niether) the [9](cheif, chief) nor his wife nor any of the [10](weird, wierd) but [11](freindly, friendly) elves who helped them had [12](reveiwed, reviewed) the list or [13](weighed, wieghed) the load to make sure that the animals could attain a [14](height, hieght) of [15](eighty, ieghty) meters. This [16](speceis, species) was known for its strength. It [17](reigned, riegned) at the top among all other creatures that pulled loads for [18](either, iether) labor or [19](leisure, liesure).

It was hard to [20](beleive, believe) that someone could climb aboard, [21](seize, sieze) the [22](reins, riens), and with [23](shreiks, shrieks) of joy, start the journey toward every [24](neighborhood, nieghborhood) in the world. One [25](peice, piece) at a time, the presents would be delivered to sleeping children.

The dark sky began to [26](receive, recieve) a thick [27](veil, viel) of clouds. Then the master himself suddenly appeared. Surely he would not [28](deceive, decieve) the waiting children. Rolling with laughter and feeling his [29](veins, viens) pulse with excitement, he climbed aboard. No son, daughter, [30](neice, niece), or nephew would be disappointed this year. Santa had arrived!

Using *a* and *an*

Learning when to use *a* and *an* may be one of the first spelling rules students learn. However, even in the upper grades, students do not always remember the rule for when to use these words. Many students have not internalized the correct sound pattern of using *an* before words that begin with a vowel or a vowel sound.

1. Identify the vowels. Write *a*, *e*, *i*, *o*, and *u* on the board. Remind students that all the other letters of the alphabet are consonants.

2. Now write two rows of vowels and add the *r*-controlled vowel symbols (see below) in the third row. (Refer to Louisa C. Moats's English Vowel Chart in her book, *LETRS: Language Essentials for Teachers of Reading and Spelling*, 2003, Module 2, page 98, for a complete visual of all the vowel sounds.)

Vowel Sounds

Short vowel sounds	ă	ĕ	ĭ	ŏ	ŭ
Long vowel sounds	ā	ē	ī	ō	
r-controlled vowel sounds	âr	êr	îr	ôr	ûr

3. Explain the rule: *Use **an** before words beginning with a vowel or a vowel sound.* Tell students: *Pay careful attention to the initial sound. Sometimes a word begins with a vowel and makes a consonant sound and vice versa.*

4. Draw breve marks (˘) above the first row of vowels. Review the short vowel sounds and use a few examples to demonstrate the rule (e.g., *an **apple**, an **igloo***).

5. Draw macrons (‐) above the second row of vowels and review the long vowel sounds. Explain to students that there is no long *u* vowel sound. Long *u* is the consonant sound of *y* /y/ followed by /o͞o/. If a word begins with the letter *u* and it makes a long *u* sound, it is preceded by the word *a*, not the word *an*.

6. Write the words *university*, *uniform*, and *used* on the board. Have students pronounce them and write each in a sentence, using both *a* and *an* as articles. Emphasize the consonant *y* /y/ sound at the beginning followed by /o͞o/, and how these words flow better when preceded with the article *a*. Tell students that words beginning with the letter *u* have a consonant *y* /y/ sound followed by /o͞o/. These words follow the rule and are preceded by the word *a*.

umbrella   **unicorn**

7. Words that begin with an *r*-controlled vowel have initial sounds that mimic *r* more than a vowel: *âr, ôr,* and *êr*. Explain to students that these are vowel sounds. Remind them that the *êr* sound has three spellings: *er, ir,* and *ur*. Words that begin with an *r*-controlled vowel sound begin with a vowel, and the word *an* precedes them.

8. Words that begin with the consonant *h* should be pronounced carefully because sometimes the *h* is silent. Write the following words on the board: *horse, habit, hare, holiday*. The sound /h/ can be heard, so the word *a* precedes each word. Now write these words: *herb, honor*. The *h* is silent and the first sound is a vowel sound, so the word *an* precedes each word.

9. Tell students that *an* also comes before words that begin with certain letters of the alphabet (the vowels *a, e, i, o, u* and the consonants *f, h, l, m, n, r, s, x*) when those letters are used individually or are referred to by name, such as in an acronym. For example: *an F in class, an AA meeting, an X ray,* and *an SOS signal*.

10. Reproduce the chart below to help students organize what they have learned.

A	AN
• /y/ followed by /o͞o/ (*university*) • Before words beginning with hard *h* sound	• Before words beginning with a vowel or a vowel sound • Before words beginning with *r*-controlled vowel sounds (*âr, ôr, êr*) • Before words beginning with an *h* when the *h* is silent • Before some letters of the alphabet when those letters are used individually (*f, h, l, m, n, r, s, x, a, e, i, o, u*)

978-1-4129-5826-4

Practice with **a** and **an**

Rule
Use *an* before words beginning with a vowel or a vowel sound.

Directions: Write *a* or *an* on the line before each word.

1. _____ student   _____ hungry student

2. _____ woman   _____ energetic woman

3. _____ eagle   _____ endangered eagle

4. _____ elephant   _____ giant elephant

5. _____ X ray   _____ blurry X ray

6. _____ professor   _____ intelligent professor

7. _____ skydiver   _____ enthusiastic skydiver

8. _____ neighbor   _____ honest neighbor

9. _____ hour   _____ long hour

10. _____ phone call   _____ urgent phone call

11. _____ umbrella   _____ huge umbrella

12. _____ fact   _____ unverified fact

13. _____ situation   _____ humorous situation

14. _____ university   _____ old university

15. _____ automobile   _____ hybrid automobile

16. _____ SOS signal   _____ faint SOS signal

17. _____ story   _____ emotional story

18. _____ game   _____ unbelievable game

19. _____ hand   _____ soft hand

20. _____ F grade   _____ disappointing F grade

More a and an Practice

Directions: Write *Yes* if the sentence is correct.
Write *No* if the sentence is incorrect.

1. _____ I drive an Infiniti.

2. _____ Do you want a candy?

3. _____ She's a excellent student.

4. _____ Luis was a honor student last month.

5. _____ Eduardo laid a book on his desk.

6. _____ Andrea carried a umbrella because it was raining.

7. _____ Monique wrote her grandmother a letter.

8. _____ Cilantro is a herb.

9. _____ Are you an honest person?

10. _____ Her sister studies hard so she can get an good education.

11. _____ I saw a eagle flying in the sky.

12. _____ Several teachers went to an health club after school.

13. _____ He wants to be an actor when he graduates from college.

14. _____ Is this an easy assignment for you?

15. _____ He has a doctor appointment this afternoon.

16. _____ A old ewe was eating the boy's shoe.

17. _____ Would you like an herbal tea before you go to bed?

18. _____ Our neighbor is an university professor.

19. _____ Their dog gained a enormous amount of weight over the summer.

20. _____ My brother's favorite show is an NBC program.

a or an Word-Sort Race

Directions: Cut out the word cards. Put the *a* card on the left side of your desk and the *an* card on the right side. Turn the other word cards facedown. At your teacher's signal, turn over the word cards and place them under *a* or *an*.

Rule
Use *an* before words beginning with a vowel or a vowel sound.

a		an	
hungry student	woman	energetic woman	endangered eagle
elephant	giant elephant	X ray	blurry X ray
professor	intelligent professor	neighbor	honest neighbor
hour	long hour	umbrella	huge umbrella
situation	humorous situation	university	old university
automobile	hybrid automobile	SOS signal	faint SOS signal
story	interesting story	game	unbelievable game
hand	soft hand	F grade	disappointing F grade

Using a or an with h and u

H
Directions: Write *a* or *an* on the line before each word or phrase.

1. _____ hairy monkey

2. _____ healthy sandwich

3. _____ honest answer

4. _____ herb

5. _____ hammer

6. _____ horse

7. _____ hallway

8. _____ half-dollar

9. _____ horror film

10. _____ Halloween party

11. _____ happy student

12. _____ hero

13. _____ heart-to-heart talk

14. _____ honor student

U
Directions: Write *a* or *an* on the line before each word or phrase.

1. _____ umbrella

2. _____ unicorn

3. _____ understanding teacher

4. _____ unicycle

5. _____ urge to eat ice cream

6. _____ united team

7. _____ urgent call

8. _____ used car

9. _____ union president

10. _____ unique talent

11. _____ university

12. _____ unhealthy snack

13. _____ urban location

14. _____ unfortunate grade

a and an in Context

Directions: Write *a* or *an* on each line.

Rule
Use *an* before words beginning with a vowel or a vowel sound.

A Thief in the House

It was [1]_____ early morning of what would become [2]_____ warm summer day. Alfredo awoke to [3]_____ awful sound—[4]_____ electric alarm clock buzzer. It was [5]_____ horrible way to start his day. He reached over and switched off the alarm. In the process, he knocked [6]_____ empty glass off of his night table. As he picked up the glass, he saw that it now had [7]_____ crack in it. It had been [8]_____ long time since he had begun [9]_____ day in such [10]_____ unbelievably bad way.

From [11]_____ pile of clothes on the floor, he selected [12]_____ off-white colored shirt and [13]_____ pair of torn blue jeans. After he searched for [14]_____ few minutes, he found [15]_____ clean pair of socks in [16]_____ open drawer. (Even for [17]_____ eleven-year-old, he knew he was not the neatest kid on the planet.) He got dressed and looked around for [18]_____ new pair of shoes that his mother had just bought him. They were gone. He knew there was [19]_____ simple explanation—the new puppy.

Maggie was [20]_____ exceptional thief when it came to shoes. Although she had never damaged [21]_____ single one, she caused [22]_____ unnecessary amount of frustration. [23]_____ shoe was typically not where it should have been. Alfredo sometimes wondered if the family had made [24]_____ error when they adopted her from [25]_____ local pound.

As Alfredo stepped outside, he smelled [26]_____ unusual number of fragrant scents from [27]_____ herb garden across the yard. [28]_____ bright blue sky, distant snow-capped mountains creating [29]_____ uneven horizon line, and [30]_____ emerald mass of fields created [31]_____ unexpected vision of beauty. The sound of [32]_____ heavy object being dropped on the ground nearby captured his attention.

There stood Maggie, [33]_____ happily wagging tail causing her whole body to shake back and forth. Alfredo's shoes lay in front of her. They were [34]_____ little wet, but otherwise undamaged. Perhaps today would not be such [35]_____ bad day after all.

Quiz 1: Using a and an

Directions: Write *a* or *an* on each line.

The Interview

As Sarah sat in [1]_____ empty admissions office at [2]_____ major university. She could hardly contain her excitement. For [3]_____ long time she had dreamed about what [4]_____ honor it would be if she could attend [5]_____ university like this one with [6]_____ agriculture program that had [7]_____ worldwide reputation. [8]_____ kind voice brought her out of her daydream.

"The Director will see you in [9]_____ minute or two. He said that he had [10]_____ important phone call to make. It won't take [11]_____ extremely long time," stated [12]_____ attractive secretary. Within [13]_____ few minutes, she returned and showed Sarah into [14]_____ large office.

[15]_____ elderly man who could only be described as handsome rose from behind [16]_____ enormous desk. In [17]_____ instant, he made her feel at home. He sometimes looked down at [18]_____ series of questions that [19]_____ intern had gathered for this occasion. But he acted more like he was having [20]_____ casual conversation than [21]_____ interview.

"I see that you were [22]_____ A student for the past two years," he smiled, as he looked at [23]_____ transcript from Sarah's high school. "[24]_____ excellent record like that is exactly what we look for in our students. I see that you have [25]_____ interest in pursuing [26]_____ career in [27]_____ area of agriculture."

Sarah gave him [28]_____ appreciative look. "Yes," she replied, "It has long been [29]_____ goal of mine. This school has always been [30]_____ institution that has appealed to me." She had [31]_____ good feeling about the way the interview was going.

After almost [32]_____ hour of talking, the director asked Sarah, "Any other questions?"

"No," replied Sarah, "I think you have provided [33]_____ answer to every question I have asked. Now I have [34]_____ idea of what to expect if I am accepted here."

"That should not be [35]_____ problem," answered the Director. Sarah left his office with [36]_____ incredibly good feeling.

Name _____ Date _____

Quiz 2: Using *a* and *an*

Directions: Write *a* or *an* on the line before each word or phrase.

1. _____ easy exam   _____ difficult exam   _____ essay exam

2. _____ yellow ribbon   _____ orange ribbon   _____ indigo ribbon

3. _____ Utah senator   _____ Idaho senator   _____ Texas senator

4. _____ CBS program   _____ NBC program   _____ ABC program

5. _____ amazing result   _____ surprising result   _____ interesting result

6. _____ okay party   _____ birthday party   _____ Yuletide party

7. _____ secret agent   _____ undercover agent   _____ foreign agent

8. _____ Asian holiday   _____ European holiday   _____ Austrian holiday

9. _____ English tea   _____ mint tea   _____ herbal tea

10. _____ dollar   _____ yen   _____ Euro

11. _____ orphan's tale   _____ knight's tale   _____ fairy tale

12. _____ unique story   _____ unbelievable story   _____ funny story

CHAPTER 2

Words with Silent Letters

Rules

- Silent *b*—after *m* and before *t*
- Silent *g*—before *n* or *m*
- Silent *h*—usually at the beginning of a word, but also silent after a vowel at the end of a word, and after *r* or *k*
- Silent *k*—at the beginning of a word before *n*
- Silent *l*—usually before *m, f,* or *k,* and in *could, should,* and *would*
- Silent *p*—when *p* begins a word and the second letter is *n, s,* or *t*
- Silent *t*—silent in words ending in *-sten* and *-stle*
- Silent *w*—at the beginning of a word before *r,* and a few other words

Consonants that are not pronounced leave many students wondering why these silent letters are included in words at all. As students complete the following activities, they will discover that although some letters are silent, they can change the meanings of some words, as well as their pronunciations (e.g., *know/now; sign/sin; hour/our*). Although a few other letters in the English language are silent, the activities in this section will focus on words with the following silent letters: *b, g, h, k, l, p, t,* and *w.*

Read aloud with students the **Words with Silent Letters List reproducible (page 25)**. Correct any mispronunciations and discuss the meanings of the words. Have students use dictionaries as references when appropriate and encourage them to say, write, and visualize each new word to reinforce learning.

Pronunciation Practice

Say It with Meaning

Write each word from the Words with Silent Letters List on a note card. Place the cards in a small paper bag. Divide the class into teams. Ask a student to draw a word from the bag and read it aloud. Then have him or her use the word in a sentence. For each correct pronunciation, award the student's team one point. Give that team an additional two points if the student uses the word correctly in a sentence. Then put the word aside. If the student pronounces the word correctly but cannot use it properly in a sentence, put the word back in the bag. Continue giving each group a turn until there are no words left in the bag.

Say It for Points

Make transparencies of the **Word Connection Chart reproducibles (pages 26–30)**. Divide the class into two groups. Put a Word Connection Chart on the overhead. Take turns calling on a student from each group as you point to the word you want him or her to say. If the student pronounces the word correctly, give his or her team one point. Change the Word Connection Chart often so students get practice pronouncing words with different silent letters.

Spelling Practice

Spelling Bee

Use words from the Word Connection Chart reproducibles (pages 26–30) for a Spelling Bee. Select the words one at a time for students to spell. Each student must say the word, spell it, and say the word again. Listen carefully to make sure students are pronouncing the words correctly. When a student misspells a word, he or she must leave the game. To keep disqualified students engaged in learning, have them test and retest each other on the words they missed. Encourage students to say, write, and visualize words as they practice.

Ball Toss Game

Give a ball to a student. Tell students that when they have the ball, they will call out a silent consonant and another student's name. For example, a student might say: *Silent l, Emily.* The student then tosses the ball to whomever he or she called upon. When students catch the ball, have them respond with a word that contains that silent letter and continue the procedure. For example, Emily might say: *Walk. Silent g, Henry.* You may wish to set a timer to limit the amount of time students have to respond. Words should not be repeated. As students call out words with silent letters, cross them off your Words with Silent Letters List reproducible (page 25) to keep track of words that have been used.

Hurray for Homophones

Divide the class into student pairs. Give each pair a Words with Silent Letters List reproducible. Let partners spend five to ten minutes circling each silent-letter word that has a homophone and writing the homophone beside it. The partners with the most number of correctly identified word pairs wins. Use the following words as a reference:

hour, our	knew, new, gnu	knight, night
knob, nob	knot, not	know, no
would, wood	wrap, rap	wreak, reek
wring, ring	write, right	wrote, rote
wry, rye	yolk, yoke	

SAMBEE (Spelling and Meaning Bee)

Write each word from the homophone pairs (see "Hurray for Homophones," page 23) on a separate index card. Place the cards in a paper bag. Divide the class into two teams. Select a word from the bag and say it aloud. Choose a student from one team to say the word, spell it, and tell what it means or use it in a sentence. Give the student's team one point for spelling the word correctly and two points for correctly identifying its meaning or using it in a sentence (for a possible three points per turn). Continue playing until all the words have been correctly spelled and defined. Keep score on the board so the teams can track their points.

Silent Letters Flip-Chart Books

Have students make flip-chart books to keep at their desks or in their binders for reference. Give each student three sheets of two different colors of paper (e.g., three green sheets and three pink sheets). Have students stack the papers so the colors alternate. Direct them to fold the papers in half, portrait style. Next, have students unfold the papers and cut along the fold. Instruct them to stack the papers again, making sure that colors are alternating. Then have students cut a wavy or V-shaped design along the long bottom edges of the stack.

Model how to arrange the papers so each sheet protrudes slightly under the next by approximately 1/4". Ask students to fold the papers along the crease and then staple their 12-page flip-chart books across the top three times to hold the pages in place. Ask them to use the first two pages to write a title and a table of contents. On the remaining pages, students will write words with silent letters.

Words with Silent Letters List

Silent *b*	Silent *g*	Silent *h*	Silent *k*
bomb (n)	assignment (n)	herb (n)	knack (n)
bomb (v)	gnarl (v)	honest (adj)	knapsack (n)
climb (v)	gnash (v)	honesty (n)	knead (v)
comb (n)	gnat (n)	honor (n)	kneel (v)
comb (v)	gnaw (v)	honor roll (n)	kneepad (n)
crumbs (n)	gnocchi (n)	honorable (adj)	knees (n)
debt (n)	gnome (n)	honoree (n)	knew (v)
doubt (n)	gnu (n)	hour (n)	knife (n)
doubt (v)	phlegm (n)	hurrah (interj)	knight (n)
dumb (adj)	resign (v)	John (n)	knit (v)
dumbfounded (v)	sign (n)	khaki (n)	knob (n)
lamb (n)		oh (interj)	knockoff (n)
limb (n)		rheumatism (n)	knockout (n)
numb (adj)		Rhine (n)	knot (n)
plumber (n)		rhinestone (n)	knothole (n)
thumb (n)		rhinoceros (n)	know (v)
		Rhode Island (n)	know-it-all (n)
		rhyme (v)	knowledge (n)
		rhythm (n)	knuckles (n)
		Thomas (n)	
		thyme (n)	

Silent *l*	Silent *p*	Silent *t*	Silent *w*
calf (n)	pneumograph (n)	bristle (n)	answer (n)
calm (adj)	pneumonia (n)	bustle (v)	sword (n)
could (v)	pseudonym (n)	castle (n)	two (adj)
folks (n)	psoriasis (n)	fasten (v)	whole (adj)
half (n)	psychedelic (adj)	glisten (v)	wrangle (v)
palm (n)	psychic (adj)	gristle (n)	wrangler (n)
salmon (n)	psychologist (n)	hasten (v)	wrap (v)
salve (n)	psychology (n)	hustle (v)	wrath (n)
should (v)	ptarmigan (n)	listen (v)	wreak (v)
stalk (n)	pteranodon (n)	moisten (v)	wreath (n)
stalk (v)	pteridology (n)	rustle (v)	wreck (v)
talk (v)	pterodactyl (n)	thistle (n)	wreckage (n)
walk (n)	pterosaur (n)	whistle (n)	wren (n)
walk (v)		whistle (v)	wrestle (v)
would (v)			wretch (n)
yolk (n)			wriggle (v)
			wring (v)
			wrinkle (n)
			wrist (n)
			wristwatch (n)
			write (v)
			wrong (adj)
			wry (adj)

Name _____   Date _____

Word Connection Chart

Rule
Silent *b* usually comes after *m* or before *t*.

Directions: Write a definition for each word or draw a picture to help you remember it. Say and visualize the spelling of each word.

Silent Letter *b*

1. thumb (n)	**2.** limb (n)	**3.** lamb (n)
4. climb (v)	**5.** crumbs (n)	**6.** debt (n)
7. comb (n)	**8.** comb (v)	**9.** dumbfounded (v)
10. plumber (n)	**11.** bomb (n)	**12.** doubt (v)

Word Connection Chart

Rule
Silent *g* usually comes before *m* or *n*.

Directions: Write a definition for each word or draw a picture to help you remember it. Say and visualize the spelling of each word.

Silent Letter *g*

1. assignment (n)	**2.** gnarl (v)	**3.** phlegm (n)	**4.** gnat (n)
5. gnaw (v)	**6.** gnome (n)	**7.** gnu (n)	**8.** resign (v)

Rule
Silent *h* usually comes at the beginning of a word, but it is also silent after a vowel at the end of a word, and after *r* or *k*.

Silent Letter *h*

1. herb (n)	**2.** hour (n)	**3.** honest (adj)	**4.** honesty (n)
5. honor (n)	**6.** hurrah (interj)	**7.** rhyme (v)	**8.** Thomas (n)

Name _____   Date _____

Word Connection Chart

Directions: Write a definition for each word or draw a picture to help you remember it. Say and visualize the spelling of each word.

Rule
Silent *k* usually comes at the beginning of a word before *n*.

Silent Letter *k*

1. knack (n)	**2.** knapsack (n)	**3.** knead (v)	**4.** kneel (v)
5. knees (n)	**6.** knife (n)	**7.** knight (n)	**8.** knit (v)
9. knob (n)	**10.** knock (v)	**11.** knot (n)	**12.** know (v)
13. knockout (n)	**14.** knowledge (n)	**15.** knuckles (n)	**16.** know-it-all (n)

Word Connection Chart

Rule
Silent *l* usually comes before *m*, *f*, or *k*, and in *could*, *should*, and *would*.

Directions: Write a definition for each word or draw a picture to help you remember it. Say and visualize the spelling of each word.

Silent Letter *l*

1. calf (n)	**2.** walk (adj)	**3.** folks (n)	**4.** half (n)
5. palm (n)	**6.** salmon (n)	**7.** yolk (n)	**8.** talk (v)

Rule
Silent *p* usually comes at the beginning of a word when the second letter is *n*, *s*, or *t*.

Silent Letter *p*

1. pneumonia (n)	**2.** pneumograph (n)	**3.** pseudonym (n)	**4.** psychedelic (adj)
5. psychic (adj)	**6.** psychology (n)	**7.** psoriasis (n)	**8.** ptarmigan (n)
9. pteranodon (n)	**10.** pterodactyl (n)	**11.** pterosaur (n)	**12.** pteridology (n)

Word Connection Chart

Directions: Write a definition for each word or draw a picture to help you remember it. Say and visualize the spelling of each word.

Silent Letter *t*

1. castle (n)	**2.** fasten (v)	**3.** glisten (v)	**4.** listen (v)
5. hustle (v)	**6.** thistle (n)	**7.** whistle (n)	**8.** rustle (v)

Rule
Silent *w* usually comes at the beginning of a word before *r*.

Silent Letter *w*

1. wrangle (v)	**2.** wrap (v)	**3.** wreak (v)	**4.** wreath (n)
5. wreck (v)	**6.** wren (n)	**7.** two (n)	**8.** wring (v)
9. wrinkle (n)	**10.** wristwatch (n)	**11.** write (v)	**12.** sword (n)

Silent *b* Review

Directions: Write the following silent *b* words in alphabetical order. Then complete each sentence with a word from the list.

Rule
Silent *b* usually comes after *m* or before *t*.

dumbfounded	plumber	climb	lamb	debt
comb	thumb	limb	crumbs	doubt

1. _____   2. _____

3. _____   4. _____

5. _____   6. _____

7. _____   8. _____

9. _____   10. _____

11. Nancy studied hard for her math test; however, she was _____ when she got her test back and saw that she received an F grade.

12. Roberto's cat liked to _____ the tree in the front yard and wait for him to come home from school.

13. During the storm, a huge _____ from the oak tree cracked and fell on the corner of the house.

14. People who save their money will not have to go into _____ when they want to go on a nice vacation.

15. The _____ repaired the leaky faucet.

16. If you are adept at growing plants, people say you have a green _____.

17. A _____ is a baby sheep.

18. "Be careful to not get cookie _____ on the floor," Mom warned.

19. They searched the area with a fine-tooth _____ to find her missing puppy.

20. There's no _____ that Ella's grades will get her into an excellent college.

Name _____ Date _____

Silent g and h Review

Rule
Silent g usually comes before n or m.

Directions: Answer the questions. Use silent g words from the Word Connection Chart (page 27) as a reference.

1. Which word has two homophones? _____

   Write them. _____ _____

2. What word is a synonym of the word *dwarf*? _____

3. What word means "to growl"? _____

4. What word means "African antelope"? _____

5. What word means "to give up"? _____

6. Name something a beaver does. _____

7. Name a tiny insect. _____

Directions: Answer the questions. Use silent h words from the Word Connection Chart (page 27) as a reference.

Rule
Silent h usually comes at the beginning of a word, but is also silent after a vowel at the end of a word, and after r or k.

8. Write the silent h words that require the article *an*.

   _____

9. Write the silent h words that require the article *a*.

   _____

10. Write the silent h word that is a homophone.

   _____

11. Use the article *an* and a silent h word in a sentence.

   _____

12. Use the article *an* and a silent h word in a sentence.

   _____

Silent k Sound-off

Directions: Say the words without the silent letter k at the beginning. (Some are words and some are partial words.) Are they pronounced as if the k were there?

    Write k at the beginning of each word. Say the words again. Which word now has a different pronunciation? Circle it. Which words have a different meaning with a silent k at the beginning? Underline them.

_____ nack   _____ night

_____ napsack   _____ now

_____ nead   _____ nockout

_____ nees   _____ nife

_____ nob   _____ new

_____ nock   _____ not

_____ nuckles   _____ nit

Directions: Choose ten words from the list above. Write each word in a sentence.

1. _____

2. _____

3. _____

4. _____

5. _____

6. _____

7. _____

8. _____

9. _____

10. _____

Silent / Scramble

Directions: Unscramble each set of letters. Write the silent *l* word on the line.

1. duclo _____

2. mansol _____

3. aflh _____

4. slokf _____

5. lacf _____

6. amlc _____

7. katl _____

8. ulsohd _____

9. lpma _____

10. dwluo _____

11. seavl _____

12. loky _____

Directions: Circle the correct word and write it on the line. How quickly can you say this tongue twister?

How much _____ _____ a woodchuck chuck,
        (wood, would)   (wood, would)

if a woodchuck _____ chuck wood?
            (coud, could)

A woodchuck _____ chuck as much _____
        (wood, would)   (wood, would)

as a woodchuck _____ chuck,
            (coud, could)

if a woodchuck _____ chuck _____.
            (coud, could)   (wood, would)

Name _____ Date _____

Silent *p* Matching

Directions: Write each silent *p* word on the line next to its meaning.

Rule
Silent *p* usually comes at the beginning of words when the second letter is *n*, *s*, or *t*.

pneumonia	psychedelic	psoriasis	pterodactyl
pneumograph	psychic	ptarmigan	pterosaur
pseudonym	psychology	pteranodon	pteridology

1. _____ the study of ferns

2. _____ the ability to be telepathic

3. _____ disease that causes inflamation in a person's lungs

4. _____ a large pterosaur with a long pointed head and a wingspan upward of six meters

5. _____ the science that deals with mental processes and behavior

6. _____ a grouse of the Northern Hemisphere with plumage that is brown or gray in summer and white in winter

7. _____ a device for recording the force and speed of chest movements during breathing

8. _____ any of various extinct flying reptiles of the Jurassic and Cretaceous periods, characterized by wings with a flap of skin supported by the very long fourth digit on each forelimb

9. _____ a fictitious name

10. _____ generating hallucinations and altered states of awareness

11. _____ a small pterosaur, mostly tailless; extinct flying reptile

12. _____ a noncontagious inflammatory skin disease that causes scaly reddish patches

Name _____   Date _____

Silent *t* Syllabication

Rule
Silent *t* is usually found in words ending with **-sten** and **-stle**.

Directions: Say each silent *t* word. Write the number of syllables for each word in the middle column. Then divide each word between syllables in the last column.

Silent *t* Words	Number of Syllables	Separated into Syllables
1. bristle	two	bris-tle
2. bustle		
3. castle		
4. gristle		
5. hustle		
6. rustle		
7. thistle		
8. whistle		
9. fasten		
10. glisten		
11. hasten		
12. listen		
13. moisten		

14. To what syllable does the silent *t* always belong? _____

Silent *w* Review

Directions: Unscramble each set of letters. Write the word on the line.

Rule
Silent *w* usually comes at the beginning of a word before *r*.

1. sathitrcww _____
2. gelwigr _____
3. wignr _____
4. rwpa _____
5. agecerkw _____
6. tarhew _____
7. nowrg _____
8. wethcr _____
9. trlwerse _____
10. lenwirk _____

Directions: Write the silent *w* word that matches each description.

11. a small brown songbird _____

12. the joint between the hand and the forearm _____

13. a line or crease on a normally smooth surface _____

14. to put words on paper _____

15. a weapon with a long blade _____

16. a miserable person _____

17. to cover _____

18. to twist _____

19. the antonym of *correct*

_____

20. timepiece worn around the wrist

_____

Silent Letter Quiz

Directions: As you read the story, circle the words that contain a silent letter.

The Silent Knight

Sir Gab-a-Lot he was not. The knight was not a talkative man, and the king's advisors claimed he was the wrong man for the job. The king knew, however, that this warrior could be trusted to listen well and to be honest when he chose to speak. While others felt that the assignment should be given to another, the king never doubted the man's ability to complete the task successfully.

For almost half a year, the king's subjects had been numb with terror. An evil gnome with magical powers had conjured up a pterodactyl from prehistoric times. The first attack on a calf had been a surprise. Soon, workers began to hear the rustle of the pterosaur's wings several times a week as it wreaked havoc on their herds. Almost all the calves and lambs had disappeared. There was no sign that the magical spell was near its end, and the king had to calm his people.

A loud knock forced the king's attention back to the present. "He has returned!" shouted an advisor at the closed chamber doors. The king hastened to his balcony. Looking down in the courtyard, he saw his loyal warrior. Although the knight had departed from the castle less than twelve hours earlier, he now kneeled before his king. The blade of his sword glistened in the fading sunlight.

"My lord," the warrior called out, "the beast has been slain!" Cheers arose from the crowd assembled in the courtyard. Wrapped in his royal robes on the balcony above, the king held up his palm to silence the crowd.

"Sir Thomas, my people and I are forever in your debt. Climb the steps to my chambers so that I may hear of your conquest. Tomorrow will be your day of honor. We will all celebrate!" Cheers broke out again, and the king smiled. He had known all along how this story would end.

CHAPTER 3

Contractions

Contractions can provide quite a challenge to students. Students frequently misspell contractions or place the apostrophe in the wrong place. Encouraging, and even requiring, students to say the three rules of contractions aloud as they complete the following activities is imperative. When students *write* the word correctly, *see* the word spelled correctly, and *say* the rule at the same time, they are activating several senses. That activation helps the spelling pattern shift from their short-term memory to long-term memory.

Three Rules of Contractions

1. Write the following words on the board: *has, is, will, had, would, are, have, not.* Write three to five contraction combinations under each word (e.g., *aren't, hasn't, haven't* under *not*). Underline the first word in each contraction to emphasize to students how it does not change. Then ask students to note how the endings are the same. Point out that the apostrophe goes where the letter or letters are missing. Stress to students that there are three rules for contractions. Have students recite the three rules three times.

2. Erase the contraction words. Write students' names on slips of paper and place them in a paper bag or box. Draw a student's name and have that student come to the board and write one contraction combination. Ask him or her to underline the first word and say the first rule. *(Keep all of the first word.)* Next, have the student explain the placement of the apostrophe by reciting the second rule. *(Place the apostrophe where the **o** should be because the apostrophe goes where the letter or letters are missing.)* If a student writes *will not = won't,* have him or her recite the third rule.

3. Emphasize that the contraction *it's* always represents the two words *it is. It's* is never a possessive word, even though *'s* is used to show possession.

4. Tell students that their "ticket out the door" (what they need to know to leave class) is to correctly recite the three rules of contractions.

Rules
1. Keep all of the first word.
2. Place the apostrophe where the letter or letters are missing.
3. There is one exception! *will not = won't*

Contraction Construction

1. Make transparencies of the **Contraction Construction** and **Construction of Won't reproducibles (pages 42–43)**. Then copy a class set of both pages and distribute them to students. Place the transparencies in sheet protectors. Write on the sheet protector with a permanent marker as you do the following activity on an overhead projector.

2. Have students look at the Contraction Construction reproducible. Ask them to use a blue highlighter (blue represents first place) to trace the line under the first word in each contraction. Point out that the apostrophe does not always go immediately after the first word. As you highlight the line under the first word on your transparency, say with students: *Keep all of the first word.*

3. Trace over the apostrophe with a yellow marker while students follow along on their reproducibles (yellow is for caution). Ask them to use caution and think about what letter or letters are missing in the second word because that is where the apostrophe goes. As you trace over the apostrophe with students, say with them: *Place the apostrophe where the letter or letters are missing.*

4. Ask students to look at the Construction of *Won't* reproducible. Explain that this reproducible demonstrates the third rule of contractions (*will + not = won't*). As you underline the words on the overhead with a blue marker and students underline the words *will not* and *won't* on their reproducibles, say with them: *There is one exception!* **will** + **not** = **won't**. As you trace over the apostrophe in yellow with students, say aloud together: *Place the apostrophe where the letter or letters are missing.*

Contraction Galaxy

Give students a copy of **Contraction Galaxy reproducible (page 44)** and review the three rules of contractions. Tell students that each star and box shows the possible contractions for each word. Point out that there are three small stars that contain only one contraction. Discuss how only certain words can be combined to form contractions. Then ask students to visualize the appropriate contraction endings for each word. For example, if the second word in a contraction combination is *will*, the ending is *apostrophe ll ('ll)*. Encourage students to memorize each contraction group and its corresponding ending. Have them keep the Contraction Galaxy reproducible in a folder for easy reference.

Catch the Contraction

Refer to the Contraction Galaxy reproducible. Say and spell a contraction (e.g., *they're*) and then call a student's name. The student must repeat the contraction, spell it, and use it in a sentence. During each turn, the student says a different contraction, spells it, and calls on another student who then repeats the contraction, spells it again, and uses it in a sentence. If a student cannot use the contraction correctly in a sentence, he or she may ask for help from a classmate. After hearing it used correctly in a sentence, the student must then repeat the sentence correctly to complete his or her turn. Next, the student says and spells a different contraction and calls on another student to continue the activity.

Variation: When students become more proficient, have them stand and use a contraction correctly in a sentence. This time, give each student only 15 seconds to complete the task. If the timer sounds before then, that student sits down, and the original student calls on another student with the same (or a different) contraction. The last student standing is the Contraction Champion.

Contraction Construction

Directions: Use a blue highlighter to trace the line under the first word in each contraction. Trace over each apostrophe with a yellow highlighter.

I am = I'm

it is = it's
he is = he's
she is = she's

you are = you're
we are = we're
they are = they're

he has = he's
she has = she's
it has = it's

you have = you've
we have = we've
they have = they've
I have = I've

could not = couldn't
had not = hadn't
did not = didn't
would not = wouldn't
should not = shouldn't
were not = weren't

I will = I'll
you will = you'll
he will = he'll
she will = she'll
it will = it'll
we will = we'll
they will = they'll

Name _____ Date _____

Construction of *Won't*

Directions: Read each sentence. Underline the word *won't* with a blue highlighter. Highlight the apostrophe in *won't* with a yellow highlighter.

Rules
1. Keep all of the first word.
2. Place the apostrophe where the letter or letters are missing.
3. There is one exception!
   will not = won't

I will not be able to go out tonight.
I won't be able to go out tonight.

You will not be eligible if you get an F.
You won't be eligible if you get an F.

Tran will not let you copy his answers.
Tran won't let you copy his answers.

Mr. Jennings will not let you pay for dinner.
Mr. Jennings won't let you pay for dinner.

It will not rain tomorrow.
It won't rain tomorrow.

Carla will not be able to attend the party.
Carla won't be able to attend the party.

Buddy will not like going to dog obedience school.
Buddy won't like going to dog obedience school.

Keisha will not run in the marathon this year.
Keisha won't run in the marathon this year.

Ms. Chang will not teach this summer.
Ms. Chang won't teach this summer.

The tree will not be cut down.
The tree won't be cut down.

Brent will not go to baseball camp next week.
Brent won't go to baseball camp next week.

Katie's mouse will not finish the maze.
Katie's mouse won't finish the maze.

Will not

won't

Contraction Galaxy

Rules
1. Keep all of the first word.
2. Place the apostrophe where the letter or letters are missing.
3. There is one exception!
   will not = won't

has = 's
it has = it's
he has = he's
she has = she's
that has = that's
there has = there's

let us = let's

is = 's
it is = it's
he is = he's
she is = she's
how is = how's
that is = that's
there is = there's
who is = who's
what is = what's
where is = where's

will = 'll
I will = I'll
we will = we'll
you will = you'll
it will = it'll
he will = he'll
she will = she'll
they will = they'll

had = 'd
I had = I'd
we had = we'd
you had = you'd
it had = it'd
he had = he'd
she had = she'd
they had = they'd

would = 'd
I would = I'd
we would = we'd
you would = you'd
it would = it'd
he would = he'd
she would = she'd
they would = they'd
who would = who'd

I am = I'm

not = n't
is not = isn't
do not = don't
does not = doesn't
are not = aren't
has not = hasn't
would not = wouldn't

have = 've
I have = I've
we have = we've
you have = you've
they have = they've

are = 're
we are = we're
you are = you're
they are = they're

will not = won't

Reproducible

Using Contractions

Directions: Write the contraction for each underlined set of words on the line.

1. I <u>will not</u> be able to go out tonight.

   _____

2. <u>He has</u> earned enough money to buy a new bike.

   _____

3. Do you know where <u>we are</u> going? _____

4. I can't believe that <u>I am</u> going to get to go to Las Vegas! _____

5. We hope it <u>will not</u> rain tomorrow. _____

6. <u>They are</u> the best spellers! _____

7. From now on, <u>he will</u> be the leader. _____

8. I <u>would not</u> do that if I were you! _____

9. She <u>should have</u> studied more often. _____

10. <u>Let us</u> go to the library now, okay? _____

Directions: What letters are replaced by apostrophes? Write the missing letters on the lines.

11. you're _____   12. they've _____

13. I'm _____   14. he's _____

15. we're _____   16. aren't _____

17. won't _____   18. doesn't _____

19. they're _____   20. let's _____

Name _____ Date _____

Contraction Action

Directions: Read the story. If a sentence contains a word combination that can be rewritten as a contraction, highlight the words. Then write the contraction on the corresponding line. If the sentence does not contain a word combination that can be rewritten as a contraction, write *No* on the corresponding line.

How the Camel Got Its Hump

[1]In the beginning of the world, when all the animals were new and beautiful, the camel was the only animal that did not want to work. [2]People gathered the animals together and said, "I am very sorry that the camel refuses to work." [3]The animals were angry that the camel was lazy and just said, "Humph!" all day.

[4]The animals told the wise man in charge of the desert that the camel did not do anything. [5]"He has not done a stroke of work. [6]He will not trot. [7]He will not plow. [8]He will not fetch. [9]He will only say, 'Humph!'"

[10]The wise man whirled himself across the desert to a pool of water and found the lazy camel, gazing at his own reflection. [11]"What is this I hear of you not doing any work?" demanded the wise man. [12]"You have given the other animals extra work because of your laziness."

[13]The camel just said, "Humph!"

[14]"I will give you a permanent humph," the wise man replied. [15]"You will be able to live without eating or drinking for many days now because of your humph." [16]The more the camel said, "Humph!" the bigger the hump on his back became. [17]And that is how the camel got his hump.

Adapted from Rudyard Kipling's Just So Stories

1. _____ 2. _____ 3. _____ 4. _____

5. _____ 6. _____ 7. _____ 8. _____

9. _____ 10. _____ 11. _____ 12. _____

13. _____ 14. _____ 15. _____ 16. _____

17. _____

Contraction Practice

Directions: Highlight the contractions in the story and list them on a separate sheet of paper. Beside each contraction write the two words used to form it.

Let's Go See Our Future

"Ta da!" I said as I tugged the cover off the time machine with a flourish. I had found it discarded in the street and had thought to myself, "Isn't this cool? I'll bet my friends would love to see this."

I looked at their awed faces. "That is so cool," squealed Megan, her dark eyes shining with excitement.

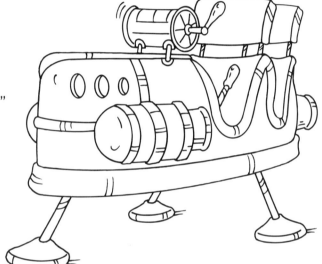

"It's cool, all right," agreed Brandi.

"I agree," said Morgan. "I can't believe it's true."

"I know," I said happily. "Who's interested in going for a ride?"

"Wouldn't miss it," cried Brandi.

"You bet I'm coming," said Morgan.

"We're all ready," agreed Megan.

We got in, and I said, "There aren't any instructions, so we'll just have to see what happens." I started to hit a few buttons.

"You're sure you know where this is going?" asked Megan.

"To the year 2020," I replied. "You'll be able to see your future self."

Suddenly, the machine gave a frightening lurch. "What's happening?" shouted my friends fearfully. "This doesn't seem right. You've got to do something."

I turned to my friends and smiled calmly, "There's nothing to worry about. I won't let anything happen to anyone." But I really couldn't know that for sure. "They'll just have to trust me," I thought, "even if I haven't got a clue." The only thing I knew for sure was that if it did work, we'd be off on the most amazing adventure of our lives.

—Submitted by Sarah E., Grade 5

Contraction Quiz

Directions: Write the correct contraction on each line.

1. who is = _____   **2.** will not = _____

3. we will = _____   **4.** what is = _____

5. let us = _____   **6.** do not = _____

7. he had = _____   **8.** she has = _____

9. who would = _____   **10.** how is = _____

Directions: Write the missing letter or letters in each contraction on the line.

11. I'm _____   **12.** I'd _____

13. doesn't _____   **14.** you're _____

15. you've _____   **16.** wouldn't _____

17. they're _____   **18.** we're _____

19. there's _____   **20.** we've _____

Directions: Read the story below. When you see a word combination that can be rewritten as a contraction, circle the words. Then write the contraction on another sheet of paper.

The Beautiful Little Bee

(line 1)   "I do not like this windy weather," the little bee complained to her mother. "The
(line 2) pollen from the flowers gets all over my face. It is everywhere."

(line 3)   "I am sorry," her mother replied. "However, we are lucky there is so much pollen.
(line 4) We will be able to make lots of delicious honey."

(line 5)   "But you are not listening! I will be embarrassed," the little bee pouted.

(line 6)   "I would not worry! The wind is strong. There will not be any pollen left on your
(line 7) beautiful face when you get home," her mother smiled gently.

CHAPTER 4

Plural Nouns

A variety of spelling rules are associated with plural nouns. Use "Making Nouns Plural" as an introductory activity to prepare students for learning the rules of spelling plural nouns. Then play the following games to teach and reinforce concepts in a way that engages students and all of their senses.

Making Nouns Plural

Draw a T-chart on the board. Write the heading *Singular Nouns* on one side and *Plural Nouns* on the other side. To assess students' prior knowledge, solicit examples of singular and plural nouns. Write the nouns under the appropriate headings. Circle the endings on the plurals. Circle the whole word if the plural noun is irregular.

Rules and Exceptions

Review the rules for making plural nouns on pages 6–7. Write the rules on the board or chart paper for students. Provide several examples for each rule and exception, if appropriate.

Make ten photocopies of the **Making Nouns Plural reproducible (page 51)** for each student. Demonstrate how to write the rule at the top and list several examples. Then write any exceptions to the rule. Repeat with another reproducible for the next rule.

Once students have completed all the rules for making nouns plural, give them a hole punch and three brass brads. Invite them to create their own "Making Nouns Plural" reference book.

Ball Toss Game

Give a ball to a student. Instruct the student to call out s*ingular* or *plural* and another student's name. For example, a student might say: *Singular, Jose.* Then have the student toss the ball to whomever he or she called upon. When a student catches the ball, have him or her respond with a word appropriate to the command and continue the procedure. For example, Jose might say: *Bird. Plural, Jessica.* As students become more proficient, give them points for answering correctly. Use a timer to limit response time. If you choose not to use a ball, simply ask students to respond when their names are called.

Rules
- Add *s* in most cases.
- Add *es* to words ending in *s, sh, ch, x,* and *z.*
- Change *f* or *fe* to *v,* and add *es.*
- Change *y* to *i* if a consonant comes before the *y,* and add *es.*
- Keep the *y* and add *s* when a vowel comes before *y.*
- Add *es* to words ending with a consonant and *o.*
- Add *s* if a vowel precedes the *o.*
- In hyphenated compound words, add *s* to the base noun.
- Some nouns have irregular plural forms.
- Some nouns have the same spelling in both singular and plural forms.

Circle and Say

Invite students to play "Circle and Say" after they have completed the activities on the **Review the Rule** and **Using Irregular Plurals reproducibles (pages 52–53)**.

Photocopy a class set of the **Circle and Say reproducible (page 54)**. Divide the class into pairs. Ask students to work with their partners to highlight the plural nouns in the story. Then have them take turns circling the plural endings with a red pen and saying the corresponding spelling rule to their partners.

When students have finished highlighting the plural nouns and identifying the plural endings, write their names and the plural nouns from the story on slips of paper. Place students' names in one paper bag and the plural nouns in another bag. Draw a student's name and ask him or her to come to the board. Have the student draw a word from the bag of plural nouns and write the word on the board. Ask the student to circle the ending with red chalk or marker and tell the class the spelling rule. Then ask him or her to draw the name of the next student and repeat the process.

Tongue Twister for Your Brain

Photocopy a class set of the **Tongue Twister for Your Brain reproducible (page 55)**. After students have completed the reproducible, try this follow-up oral activity. Students do not need any materials. Divide the class into two teams. Have a Tongue Twister for Your Brain reproducible handy as a reference. Say aloud the singular nouns and give one student from each team only a short time (five seconds) to say all the corresponding plural nouns. For example, you might say: *Wish, child, boy,* and the student might respond: *Wishes, children, boys.* Award teams one point for each correct plural for a possible three points per turn.

wishes, children, boys

Making Nouns Plural

Directions: Review the rules for making nouns plural. Complete the graphic organizer for each rule.

Rule

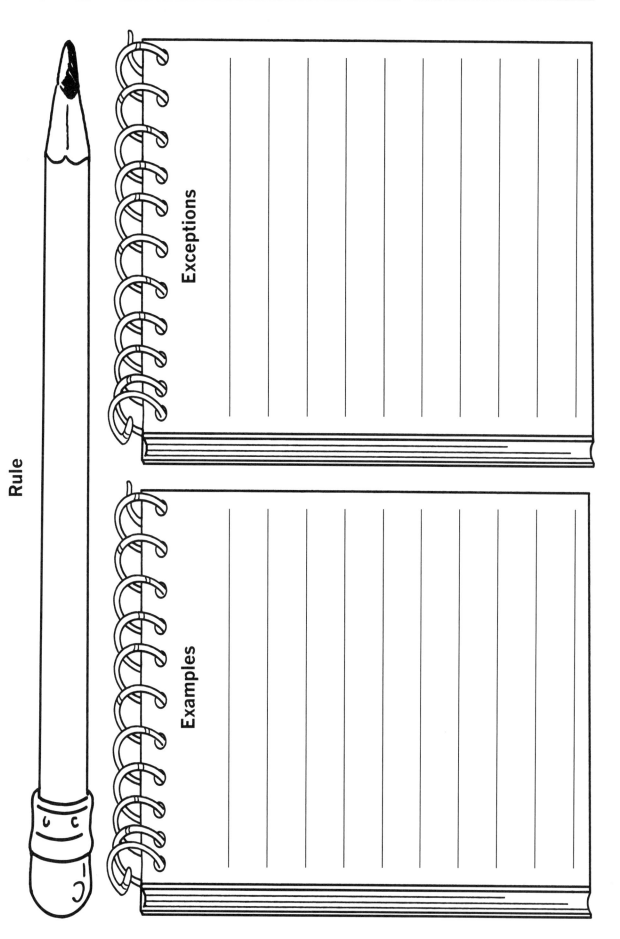

Exceptions

Examples

Name _____ Date _____

Review the Rule

Rules
- Add *s* in most cases.
- Add *es* to words ending in *s*, *sh*, *ch*, *x*, and *z*.

Directions: Write *s* or *es* to make these words plural. Then write the plural word.

1. witch + _____ = _____

2. coat + _____ = _____

3. glass + _____ = _____

4. table + _____ = _____

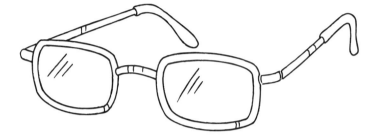

5. speech + _____ = _____   6. fox + _____ = _____

7. flag + _____ = _____   8. princess + _____ = _____

9. wish + _____ = _____   10. sphinx + _____ = _____

11. bench + _____ = _____   12. steak + _____ = _____

13. dish + _____ = _____   14. fax + _____ = _____

Directions: If you change the *y* to *i*, write *yes* on the line. If not, write *no*. Then write the plural word.

Rules
- Change *y* to *i* when a consonant comes before the *y*, and add *es*.
- Keep the *y* and add *s* when a vowel comes before *y*.

15. valley _____ = _____

16. baby _____ = _____

17. boy _____ = _____

18. spy _____ = _____

19. country _____ = _____   20. key _____ = _____

21. toy _____ = _____   22. berry _____ = _____

23. freeway _____ = _____   24. city _____ = _____

25. sky _____ = _____   26. tray _____ = _____

27. story _____ = _____   28. dairy _____ = _____

Name _____ Date _____

Using Irregular Plurals

Directions: Write the correct plural noun for each singular noun.

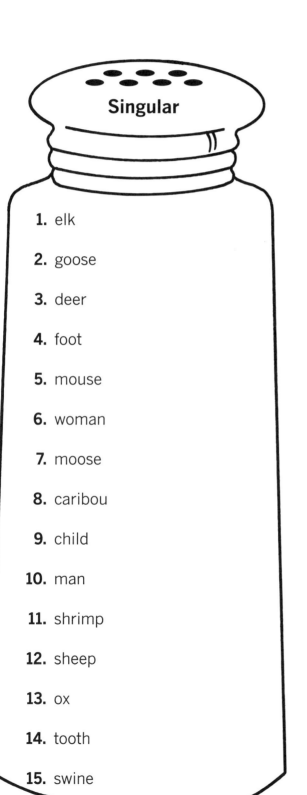

Singular

1. elk
2. goose
3. deer
4. foot
5. mouse
6. woman
7. moose
8. caribou
9. child
10. man
11. shrimp
12. sheep
13. ox
14. tooth
15. swine

Plural

1. _____
2. _____
3. _____
4. _____
5. _____
6. _____
7. _____
8. _____
9. _____
10. _____
11. _____
12. _____
13. _____
14. _____
15. _____

Name _____   Date _____

Circle and Say

Directions: Highlight each plural noun in the story with a yellow highlighter. Then circle the plural ending with red pen. Say the spelling rule to your partner.

A Good Beginning

Children boarded the buses like sheep following their leaders. Women from schools that had planned this trip watched and chattered like monkeys. They expressed their beliefs about what should take place next. Some gave dramatic speeches about events that might threaten the "little babies" as they passed through dangerous cities along the freeways the students would travel. Two men and their wives who were going along with the young boys and girls made promises to satisfy everyone's wishes as much as possible. Then any echoes of doubt died away.

Parents filled the cargo bays of the buses with a few final boxes filled with loaves of bread, batches of sandwiches, and containers of strawberries. Then they closed the storage hatches. Drivers checked their watches and turned their keys in the ignition switches of their coaches. Remaining moms stepped back a few feet. Some were fluttering their eyelashes to keep the tears in their eyes. They blew kisses to their loved ones. The trip had begun.

As they headed south for the first time in most of their lives, the little travelers looked out the windows at the passing hills and valleys. It was too late in the day to see deer or foxes, but a number of newborn calves were seen along the route. A boy with glasses and his sister lowered the window and began to sniff the smells of the countryside like little mice. In the front of the same bus, the driver winced as a few butterflies splattered against his windshield, creating ugly messes. He quickly switched on the wipers and washed away the bodies before any of the little princes or princesses onboard noticed. Many exciting days, places, and journeys lay ahead for the youngsters. A good start to such a trip was always important.

Tongue Twister for Your Brain

Directions: Write the plural form of each word. Say and visualize each noun as you write it.

1. wish, child, boy _____ _____ _____

2. monkey, sheep, wolf _____ _____ _____

3. goose, toy, bush _____ _____ _____

4. life, day, moose _____ _____ _____

5. turkey, man, hoof _____ _____ _____

6. dish, species, key _____ _____ _____

7. elf, foot, country _____ _____ _____

8. lunch, lady, deer _____ _____ _____

9. branch, mouse, balloon _____ _____ _____

10. tooth, ladder, leaf _____ _____ _____

11. spider, ox, witch _____ _____ _____

12. woman, tiger, bunch _____ _____ _____

13. eye, cloud, wife _____ _____ _____

14. room, sheep, switch _____ _____ _____

15. moose, light, box _____ _____ _____

16. book, tooth, loaf _____ _____ _____

17. fox, deer, star _____ _____ _____

18. recess, hotel, woman _____ _____ _____

19. ox, business, calf _____ _____ _____

20. child, bicycle, tax _____ _____ _____

Plural Nouns Quiz

Directions: Write singular nouns. Then write the plural form of the nouns.

Nouns ending in *s*	Nouns ending in *sh*	Nouns ending in *ch*
bus—buses	wish—wishes	speech—speeches
1. _____	6. _____	11. _____
2. _____	7. _____	12. _____
3. _____	8. _____	13. _____
4. _____	9. _____	14. _____
5. _____	10. _____	15. _____

Nouns ending in *x*	Nouns ending in *f* or *fe*	*y* after a consonant
fax—faxes	loaf—loaves	country—countries
16. _____	21. _____	26. _____
17. _____	22. _____	27. _____
18. _____	23. _____	28. _____
19. _____	24. _____	29. _____
20. _____	25. _____	30. _____

y after a vowel	Nouns with irregular plural forms	Nouns that are the same in singular and plural forms
monkey—monkeys	child—children	deer—deer
31. _____	36. _____	41. _____
32. _____	37. _____	42. _____
33. _____	38. _____	43. _____
34. _____	39. _____	44. _____
35. _____	40. _____	45. _____

CHAPTER 5

Prefixes

When students learn to use morphemic strategies effectively, they become better spellers and readers. When students can break apart a word into smaller pieces and understand the function and meaning of each piece, they are empowered to use higher-level vocabulary and spell words correctly.

Three Rules of Adding Prefixes

Teach students the three rules of adding prefixes. Read the rules aloud while students read along silently. Provide opportunities for students to rehearse the rules repeatedly—aloud, silently, and in writing—to aid in retention.

Give students a copy of the **Prefix List reproducible (page 59)**. Review the list with students to help them remember the prefixes and their meanings. Sometimes students get confused when the prefix ends with the same letter that begins the base word (e.g., *irregular, illegal, immoral*). Students tend to think that one of the double letters should be dropped. During the following activities, remind students repeatedly of the first rule of prefixes—base word spellings do not change.

Rules

- When adding prefixes, the spelling of the base word does not change.
- Sometimes a hyphen separates the prefix and the base word.
- Use a hyphen before a capital letter.

Word Search

Have students fold a sheet of paper into eighths. This will give them eight boxes on each side for a total of 16 boxes. Give students a set amount of time to read through a self-selected book for 20 to 30 minutes to find words with prefixes.

The first time students find a word with a prefix, they should write the prefix in the top section of one of the boxes and then write the word containing that prefix under it. Students will be able to keep track of 16 lists of words with different prefixes. When they are finished, solicit examples of words with prefixes and write them on the board. Circle the prefix in each word to show that the spelling of each base word does not change to accommodate the prefix.

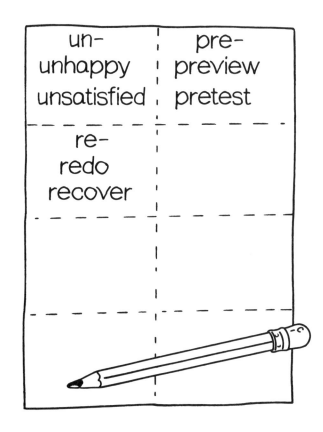

SAMBEE (Spelling and Meaning Bee)

Refer to the **Prefix Words and Meanings reproducible (page 60)**. Write each word on the front of an index card. Write the definition on the back. Place the cards in a resealable plastic bag. Then divide the class into two teams. Select a word from the bag and say it aloud. Tell the part of speech to give students a clue to the word's meaning (e.g., *forehead; noun*).

Choose a student from one team and ask him or her to say the word, spell it, and tell what it means. Students must spell the words correctly using their knowledge of the spelling rules for adding prefixes to base words. You may wish to help students with the spelling of base words, but all students must know how to spell the prefixes and be able to say the first few letters of the base word.

Give a student's team two points for spelling the word correctly and two points for giving the correct meaning of the word (for a possible total of four points). If you have struggling students, you may wish to modify the way they earn points. For example, give two points for correctly spelling the prefix and only the first few letters of the base word. Add an additional two points per turn if students are able to spell the entire word (for a possible four points for spelling only). Keep score on the board so teams can track their points.

You may wish to photocopy a class set of the Prefix Words and Meanings reproducible so students can study before you play SAMBEE. Or have students help you make a new list of prefix words to use in the game.

Circle the Prefix Words

Copy a class set of the **Circle the Prefix Words reproducible (page 61)**. Before students complete the reproducible independently, teach the difference between the prefix *il-* meaning *not*, and the word *ill* meaning *not well* or *bad*, found in hyphenated compound words such as *ill-mannered*. The prefix *il-* is spelled with only one *l*.

Prefix List

Prefix	Meaning
un-	not, opposite of
re-	again
in-, im-, ir-, il-	not
dis-	not, opposite of
en-, em-	cause to
non-	not
in-, im-	in or into
over-	too much
mis-	wrongly
sub-	under
pre-	before
inter-	between, among
fore-	before
de-	opposite of
trans-	across
super-	above
semi-	half
anti-	against
mid-	middle
under-	too little
pro-	in favor of
ex-	out, away

Prefix Words and Meanings

Prefix *pre-*, meaning *before*	Prefix *fore-*, meaning *before*
precaution (n): action taken in advance to protect against possible danger **precede (v):** to come, exist, or occur before **preclude (v):** to make impossible by taking action in advance **pre-Columbian (adj):** originating in the Americas before the arrival of Columbus **preconceive (v):** to form an opinion before possessing knowledge or experience **predate (v):** to mark or designate with a date earlier than the actual one **predetermine (v):** to determine in advance **predict (v):** to tell about in advance **preface (n):** introductory section of a speech or book **prefix (n):** morphograph placed at the front of a word	**forecast (v):** to predict something in advance **forefather (n):** ancestor **forefoot (n):** either of the front feet of a quadruped **foreground (n):** part of a scene or picture nearest and in front of the viewer **forehand (adj):** made or done with the hand moving forward **forehead (n):** part of the face between the eyebrows and the hairline **foreman (n):** man who leads a work crew **foreshadow (v):** to suggest beforehand **forethought (n):** plan or thought beforehand **foreword (n):** preface or introductory note for a book
Prefix *im-*, meaning *not*	Prefix *ir-*, meaning *not*
immobile (adj): fixed; immovable **immodest (adj):** lacking modesty **immoral (adj):** contrary to established moral principles **immortal (adj):** not subject to death **immovable (adj):** impossible to move **immune (adj):** not subject to an obligation imposed on others **impassable (adj):** impossible to pass **impatient (adj):** not patient **impolite (adj):** not polite; discourteous **improper (adj):** not proper	**irreconcilable (adj):** not able to reconcile **irredeemable (adj):** not able to redeem or reform **irrefutable (adj):** not able to refute or disprove **irregular (adj):** contrary to rule or general practice **irremovable (adj):** not able to remove **irreplaceable (adj):** not able to replace **irresistible (adj):** not able to resist **irresponsible (adj):** not responsible **irreversible (adj):** not able to reverse **irrevocable (adj):** not able to retract or revoke

Name _____ Date _____

Circle the Prefix Words

Directions: Read the following story. Circle the words with a prefix. Write the words on the lines below. Then write what each word means.

A Boisterous Birthday

    I gazed through the restaurant window and saw a scene that was totally illogical. Customers were not sitting quietly at their tables eating dinner. They were yelling and stuffing themselves. Everyone was overeating! They were yelling at each other and grabbing food off other customers' tables. One unfriendly man was so ill-mannered that he took the birthday cake from a child's table right after the family finished singing "Happy Birthday." This was no misunderstanding. Unfortunately, it put all the children in an unhappy mood. The greedy man had underestimated the displeasure he was causing. The children were beginning to cry. But an unflustered parent saved the day. Just like a superhero, he recovered the cake and took the children from the restaurant. They left the other immature, overindulging guests to eat to their heart's content.

1. _____ = _____
2. _____ = _____
3. _____ = _____
4. _____ = _____
5. _____ = _____
6. _____ = _____
7. _____ = _____
8. _____ = _____
9. _____ = _____
10. _____ = _____
11. _____ = _____
12. _____ = _____
13. _____ = _____

Name _____ Date _____

Write the Word That Means . . .

Directions: Write the word with a prefix that matches each definition.

1. _____ not protected

2. _____ to gain again

3. _____ not proven

4. _____ opposite of *like*

5. _____ not moral

6. _____ not regular

7. _____ not legal

8. _____ to carry across

9. _____ across the Atlantic

10. _____ not friendly

11. _____ to act among each other

12. _____ to state something incorrectly

13. _____ a way underground

14. _____ middle of the night

15. _____ a hero, above and beyond

16. _____ to eat too much

17. _____ too protective

18. _____ half a circle

19. _____ to estimate too low

20. _____ opposite of *equal*

21. _____ to spell incorrectly

22. _____ opposite of *approve*

23. _____ to write again

24. _____ to pay too much

25. _____ not human

26. _____ to plan before

27. _____ not making sense

28. _____ not possible

29. _____ across the continent

30. _____ not rational

Prefix Quiz

Directions: Write the word with a prefix that matches each definition.

1. _____ not happy

2. _____ a highway between states

3. _____ not polite

4. _____ to tell something in advance

5. _____ impossible to revoke

6. _____ impossible to refute

7. _____ to communicate wrongly

8. _____ not satisfied

9. _____ to estimate too low

10. _____ to occur in the middle of the summer

11. _____ to view beforehand

12. _____ before the time of Columbus

13. _____ to speak in error

14. _____ impossible to recover

15. _____ not patient

16. _____ not proper

17. _____ to do again

18. _____ to start again

19. _____ to put in the wrong place

20. _____ a thought beforehand

CHAPTER 6

Suffixes

Spelling words with suffixes creates challenges for students because of the many different rules to remember. Emphasize to students the important tasks that suffixes perform. Suffixes can create nouns, change some words to adjectives, and change the tense of verbs. The suffix -*ness*, meaning *that which is*, changes an adjective to a noun (e.g., *happy/happiness*). The suffix -*ful*, meaning *full of*, changes a noun to an adjective (e.g. *joy/joyful*). Adding -*ed* to a word transforms it into an adjective or changes a verb to past tense (e.g., *lighted candle; jumped*).

Seven Rules of Suffixes

There are seven basic rules for adding suffixes. Review the rules provided on page 7. Write the rules on chart paper or create a bulletin board for student reference. Provide several examples for each rule and exceptions, if appropriate.

For maximum learning, set aside seven weeks to cover the rules for adding suffixes. Teach one rule per week, and spend ten minutes per day practicing and reviewing it. Each week give students a copy of the **Adding Suffixes Rules reproducible (page 66)**. Demonstrate how to complete the graphic organizer by writing the rule at the top of the page. Then write numerous examples and encourage students to add their own. Record any exceptions to the rule at the bottom of the page.

Throughout the unit, stop periodically and review previous suffix rules. Use quick, informal assessments such as asking students to write or recite the rules with several examples. At the end of the unit, have students staple together all seven reproducibles to make a handy reference book.

Rules
- Drop the final *e* when the suffix begins with a vowel.
- Keep the final *e* when the suffix begins with a consonant.
- Keep the final *e* when it is preceded by a vowel in the base word.

Final *e* Rules

After students have completed the **Final e Rules reproducible (page 67)**, have them study the new words that they have written. Point out that the vowel sound of the base word is still a long vowel sound and that there is only one consonant letter before the suffix. Have students highlight the vowel that makes a long vowel sound. Then have students circle the one consonant before the suffix with a red pen. As they do this, encourage students to say aloud all the words that dropped the final *e* before adding the suffix that began with a vowel.

Doubling Rules

In order to learn when to double the consonant for adding a suffix, students must know certain spelling patterns. Review long vowel sounds and the final *e* rules. Then teach the CVC (consonant-vowel-consonant) spelling pattern. Explain that if words end with a consonant, the syllable is closed and the vowel sound is short (e.g., *stop, skip*).

Students must also be able to count syllables. Have students clap with you to count syllables in the following words: *jog, slip, fan, shop*. When students understand that these are closed, one-syllable words, identify the endings by writing *CVC* over the last three letters. When students can recognize one-syllable words that end with CVC, teach the doubling rules. Tell students to double the last consonant when all three of the following conditions apply:

- The word has one syllable.

- The word ends with CVC.

- The suffix begins with a V (vowel).

Draw a chart on the board. Ask students to think of examples to practice applying these rules. Use this table as a model for your chart.

Rules
- Double the last consonant when a one-syllable word ends with CVC (consonant-vowel-consonant) and the suffix begins with a V (vowel).
- Extension: Also true when a multisyllabic word ends with CVC (i.e., *cur, fer, gin, mit, pel*) and the suffix begins with a V.

Base Word	Rule 1 Does it have one syllable?	Rule 2 Does it end in a CVC pattern?	Suffix	Rule 3 YES, suffix begins with a V (vowel).	NO, suffix does not begin with a V (vowel).	If YES for 1, 2, 3, double the final C (consonant).	Do not double the final C (consonant).
1. skip	yes	yes	-ed	yes		skipped	
2. run	yes	yes	-ing	yes		running	
3. jump	yes	no	-ing	yes			jumping
4. joy	yes	yes	-ful		no		joyful

Give students a copy of the **Using Double Consonants reproducible (page 68)**. Have them practice applying the doubling rules independently.

The extension to the one-syllable rule occurs when a word ends with a one-syllable CVC morphograph (i.e., *cur, fer, gin, mit, pel*). These multisyllable words (e.g., *recurred, permitting, compelled*) also follow the doubling rule. Teach the extension only after students have mastered the doubling rule and can apply it to one-syllable words.

Name _____ Date _____

Adding Suffixes Rules

Directions: Write the rule for adding suffixes in the ruler. Provide examples and exceptions in the chart below.

Rule

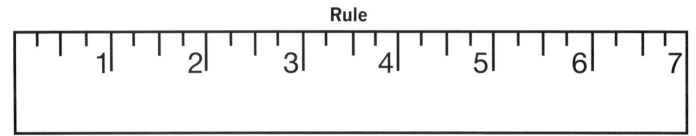

◯	Examples	Exceptions
◯		

Reproducible

Final e Rules

Directions: Add the suffix to each word. Write the new word.

1. hike + ed = _____

2. ride + ing = _____

3. bake + ing = _____

4. serve + ing = _____

Rules
- Drop the final e when the suffix begins with a vowel.
- Keep the final e when the suffix begins with a consonant.
- Keep the final e when it is preceded by a vowel in the base word.

5. face + ing = _____   6. trace + ed = _____

7. dine + ing = _____   8. write + ing = _____

9. use + ing = _____   10. fake + ed = _____

Directions: Write *yes* if the word is spelled correctly. Write *no* if it is not.

11. love + able = loveable _____   12. grade + ing = gradeing _____

13. serve + ing = serving _____   14. face + less = faceless _____

15. believe + ing = believeing _____   16. use + ed = useed _____

17. trace + ed = traced _____   18. write + ing = writing _____

19. dine + ing = dineing _____   20. wide + er = wideer _____

Final e Rules Review
Directions: Add the suffix to each word. Write the new word.

21. make + ing = _____   22. care + less = _____

23. bee + s = _____   24. name + ed = _____

25. use + ful = _____   26. wide + est = _____

27. live + able = _____   28. dine + s = _____

29. name + less = _____   30. hope + ful = _____

Using Double Consonants

<table>
<tr><td>

Rule
Double the last consonant when:
- the word has one syllable.
- the word ends with CVC.
- the suffix begins with a V (vowel).

</td></tr>
</table>

Directions: On the line beside each word, write the number of syllables you hear in the word. Circle the words with one syllable.

1. paper _____   2. wait _____

3. book _____   4. listen _____

5. tip _____   6. umbrella _____

7. think _____   8. computer _____

9. treasure _____   10. sip _____

Directions: Write a *C* for consonant or *V* for vowel above each of the last three letters of each word. Then highlight the words that end in a CVC pattern.

11. stop   12. skip

13. look   14. jump

15. dig   16. play

17. start   18. smile

19. eat   20. stir

Directions: Add the suffix to each word. Write the new word.

21. trap + ed = _____   22. play + ful = _____

23. stop + ing = _____   24. skip + ed = _____

25. joy + ful = _____   26. think + er = _____

27. nap + ing = _____   28. sit + ing = _____

29. sink + ing = _____   30. skip + er = _____

Changing *y* to *i*

Directions: Add the suffix to each word.

> **Rule**
> Change *y* to *i* when a word ends in a consonant and *y*, and the suffix is anything but *-ing*.

1. study + ing = _____

2. hurry + ed = _____

3. shy + ness = _____

4. sturdy + ness = _____

5. busy + ly = _____

6. cry + er = _____

7. try + ing = _____

8. worry + ing = _____

9. empty + ing = _____

10. copy + ed = _____

Directions: Add the suffix to each word.

> **Rule**
> Keep the *y* when a word ends in a vowel and *y*, and the suffix is *-ing*.

11. betray + s = _____

12. play + ing = _____

13. play + ful = _____

14. boy + ish = _____

15. stay + ing = _____

16. buy + ing = _____

17. spray + ed = _____

18. lay + ing = _____

19. joy + ful = _____

20. convey + s = _____

Adding Suffixes Rules Review
Directions: How many rules can you remember? Add the suffix to each word.

21. shine + ing = _____

22. happy + ness = _____

23. stop + ed = _____

24. say + ing = _____

25. want + ed = _____

26. write + ing = _____

27. skip + ed = _____

28. joy + ful = _____

29. big + est = _____

30. fancy + ful = _____

31. short + est = _____

32. hope + ed = _____

Add-a-*k* Rule

Directions: Add the suffix to each word.

1. Add -*ing* to picnic _____

2. Add -*y* to colic _____

3. Add -*y* to garlic _____   **4.** Add -*y* to gimmic _____

5. Add -*ing* to panic _____   **6.** Add -*ing* to mimic _____

7. Add -*ed* to traffic _____   **8.** Add -*ed* to panic _____

Directions: Write *yes* if the underlined word is spelled correctly. Write *no* if it is incorrect.

_____ **9.** We went <u>picnicing</u> in the park on Saturday.

_____ **10.** The baby was crying all the time because it was <u>colicky</u>.

_____ **11.** The tourists <u>paniced</u> when their boat started to sink.

_____ **12.** The young boy was <u>mimicking</u> every move his older brother made.

_____ **13.** The bread at the restaurant was really <u>garlicy</u>.

_____ **14.** The hotel guests were <u>panicking</u> because the storm knocked out the lights.

_____ **15.** During the summer, they <u>picnicked</u> together every weekend.

_____ **16.** The magician used many <u>gimmicy</u> objects to deceive his audience.

_____ **17.** Eat breath mints if your breath is <u>garlicky</u>.

_____ **18.** We laughed when he <u>mimiced</u> how his dog walked.

_____ **19.** A police officer is responsible for <u>trafficking</u> that intersection.

_____ **20.** Popular comedians are often good <u>mimickers</u>.

Name _____ Date _____

The *en* Rule

Rule
When a word ends with *w*, add the suffix -*en*, and drop the *e*.

Directions: Add -*en* to each word. Write the new word on the line.

1. blow + en = _____

2. grow + en = _____

3. know + en = _____

4. flow + en = _____

5. show + en = _____

6. sow + en = _____

7. mow + en = _____

8. throw + en = _____

Directions: Write *yes* if the underlined word is spelled correctly. Write *no* if it is incorrect.

_____ **9.** She had <u>growen</u> six inches since I last saw her.

_____ **10.** Her brother has <u>flowen</u> to Italy many times.

_____ **11.** The gardeners have <u>mowen</u> the lawn.

_____ **12.** The magician had <u>shown</u> the audience how to do one of his tricks.

_____ **13.** The storm was so fierce it had <u>blowen</u> down the tree in the front yard.

_____ **14.** The pitcher had <u>thrown</u> six strikes in a row to win the baseball game.

_____ **15.** I have <u>known</u> my best friend since first grade.

Adding Suffixes Rules Review
Directions: Add the suffixes to make new words. Write the rules that helped you spell the words correctly.

Base Word	Suffix	New Word	Rule
16. grow	-en		
17. picnic	-er		
18. cry	-ing		
19. party	-es		
20. blur	-ed		
21. bake	-ing		

al to the Rescue!

Directions: Add the suffix -al to each word before adding the suffix -ly.

Rule
When a word ends with *ic*, add *al* before adding the suffix -*ly*.

Exception: *public/publicly*

1. automatic + ly = _____

2. scientific + ly = _____

3. logic + ly = _____   **4.** enthusiastic + ly = _____

5. basic + ly = _____   **6.** frantic + ly = _____

7. music + ly = _____   **8.** magic + ly = _____

Directions: Write *yes* if the underlined word is spelled correctly. Write *no* if it is incorrect.

_____ **9.** Debate team members are good speakers who are <u>academically</u> inclined.

_____ **10.** After it rained, a rainbow <u>magicly</u> appeared in the sky.

_____ **11.** Mr. Kline <u>frantically</u> searched for his keys.

_____ **12.** The wet dog <u>patheticly</u> trudged through the rain.

_____ **13.** Exercising <u>aerobically</u> is good for your heart.

_____ **14.** The movie that won the award for Best Picture was <u>critically</u> acclaimed.

_____ **15.** Dictionary entries are ordered <u>alphabeticly</u>.

Directions: Write two sentences containing *al* words from the list above.

16. _____

_____

17. _____

_____

The *ion/or* Rule

Directions: Look at each word in the left column. If you can add the suffix -*ion* to make a new word, write it in the middle column. Then write the corresponding *er* or *or* word in the right column. The first two words are done for you.

Base Word	*ion* Word?	*or* or *er* Ending?
1. instruct	instruction	instructor
2. design	no	designer
3. project		
4. educate		
5. plant		
6. inject		
7. invent		
8. act		
9. direct		
10. speak		
11. inspect		
12. photograph		
13. help		
14. celebrate		
15. sing		

Using er and or

Directions: Are you a Super Speller? Circle the correctly spelled words ending in *or*. Trace the path of the words to find the secret letter.

> **Rule**
> If a form of the word ends in *ion*, the word is spelled with an *or* ending.

acter	mothor	washor	professer	shoppor
helper	runner	hiker	eater	saver
worker	detector	injector	projector	runnor
spender	baker	reader	eator	dictator
celebrator	drivor	father	protecter	bakor
actor	finder	workor	trappor	dancer
elector	paintor	batter	chattor	directer
imitator	sleeper	splender	mixor	rapper
collector	challengor	painter	founder	dancor
studier	compressor	inspector	evaluator	electer
compresser	teacher	movor	slippor	visor
pallor	hunter	diner	challenger	realtor
studior	mover	slipper	huntor	motivator
concentrater	dinor	whaler	swimmer	contractor
helpor	writor	docter	playor	director
sweepor	rider	teachor	motivater	instructor
confessor	evaluater	cleaner	crawlor	driver
workor	transgressor	tractor	professor	bikor
sleepor	ridor	predicter	shopper	inventer
contracter	imitater	walkor	viser	walker

Suffixes Quiz

Directions: Each word in parentheses relates to one of the rules for adding suffixes. Write the letter of the corresponding rule. Then write the new word with the suffix.

A. Final *e* Rules	C. Ending *y* Rules	E. *en* Rule	G. *ion/or* Rule
B. Doubling Rules	D. Add-a-*k* Rule	F. *al* Rule	

1. The student was (hope + *ful*) that he would get an A on the test.

Rule: _____ Word: _____

2. Kendra (panic + *ed*) when she arrived home and her front door was open.

Rule: _____ Word: _____

3. During the construction of the new building, an (inspect + *er* or *or*) was often present.

Rule: _____ Word: _____

4. The wind was so strong that several trees had (blow + *en*) down.

Rule: _____ Word: _____

5. We saw many deer tracks while (jog + *ing*) in the wilderness.

Rule: _____ Word: _____

6. At the show, the magician (magic + *ly*) pulled a rabbit out of a tall black hat.

Rule: _____ Word: _____

7. When the electricity went out, Jackson began (write + *ing*) by candlelight.

Rule: _____ Word: _____

8. The young boy was (skip + *ing*) stones on the lake with his grandfather.

Rule: _____ Word: _____

9. Mia (hurry + *ed*) home after school to play with her new puppy.

Rule: _____ Word: _____

10. The principal arranged for the famous (act + *er* or *or*) to visit the school.

Rule: _____ Word: _____

CHAPTER 7

Homophones

Rule
Homphones sound the same but have different meanings and spellings.

The homophones on the **Homophones List reproducibles (pages 79–80)** represent just a fraction of the roughly 2,000 homophones in the English language. It is no wonder that students often confuse one spelling for another.

Homophones are pronounced the same but have different meanings and spellings. *Homonyms* are words that have the same sound and the same spelling but different meanings, as in *bank* (land at the edge of a body of water) and *bank* (a place where money is kept).

Complete the "Introducing Homophones" activity to assess prior knowledge and refresh students' memories regarding homophones. Photocopy the Homophones List reproducibles for students to use as references as they complete the following activities.

Introducing Homophones

Look at the homophones on the Homophones List reproducibles. Select several words and write them on separate 5" x 7" index cards. Put the cards aside. Create sentences that emphasize the homophones. As you say the sentences, show students the corresponding index cards. Point out how the context of a homophone changes its spelling even though the pronunciation stays the same.

Encourage students to think of other homophone pairs and create their own sentences. Write the pairs on the board as students say them. Remind students that homophones are words that sound the same but have a different meanings and spellings.

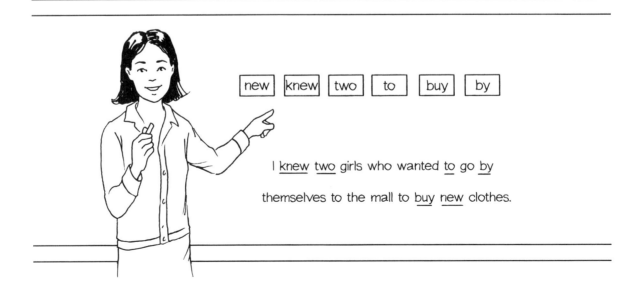

new | knew | two | to | buy | by

I <u>knew</u> <u>two</u> girls who wanted <u>to</u> go <u>by</u>
themselves to the mall to <u>buy</u> <u>new</u> clothes.

Word Wall

Post the index cards you used in the "Introducing Homophones" activity to begin a Homophones Word Wall. You may wish to post the cards with small illustrations to help clarify their meanings. Each day, write new homophones on index cards and add them to the Word Wall.

What's My Homophone?

Pin an index card with a homophone written on it to each student's back. Students must figure out their words by asking questions with a "yes" or "no" answer. Category questions work best. (Am I a liquid? Am I a verb? Am I a person? Am I an animal?) Tell students that letter hints are not allowed. (Does my word begin with the letter **s**?) As students guess their homophones, pin the cards to the Word Wall and leave space for each homophone's partner to be placed next to it.

SAMBEE (Spelling and Meaning Bee)

Refer to the Homophones List reproducibles (pages 79–80). Write about 30 homophone pairs (or trios) on separate squares of paper and place them in a paper bag. Divide the class into two groups. Select a square from the bag and read the words. Choose one of the homophones and say a sentence that uses it correctly. Choose a student from one group and ask him or her to say the word, spell it, and tell what it means. Give the student's team one point for spelling the word correctly and two points for correctly identifying its meaning or using it in a sentence (for a possible three points per turn). Continue playing until all the words have been correctly spelled and defined. Keep score on the board so teams can track their points. As you play, put each card back in the bag until you have used all the words in each homophone set. (Hint: Keep track of which homophones you have used by jotting them down as you use them in sentences.)

Homophone Tag

Write 15 pairs (or trios) of homophones on the board. Have students stand. Choose one student to be "It" and start the activity. Have "It" select a homophone from the board, slowly spell the word, and then call on another student. That student must say the same homophone, spell it again, and use it in a sentence. If the student uses the homophone correctly, he or she may sit down. "It" then selects another homophone, slowly spells it, and calls on a different student to say the homophone, spell it, and use it correctly in a sentence. Repeat the process until someone misuses a homophone in a sentence. The student who misuses a homophone becomes "It" and continues until someone else makes a mistake. Put a checkmark beside each homophone as it is used correctly. Erase homophone pairs (or trios) when they have all been used correctly in a sentence.

Homophone Challenge

Divide the class into groups of two. Ask each student to prepare his or her own paper by writing the numbers *1–20*. Have partners sit opposite each other, back-to-back. Then explain how to play the game. You will say a homophone aloud. Students must each write their own sentence using the word. The challenge is that each student in the pair must use a different form of the homophone. If the students write different forms, they get one point. The team with the most points wins.

Homophones List

Rule
Homophones sound the same but have different meanings and spellings.

ad/add
ail/ale
air/heir
all/awl
allowed/aloud
altar/alter
ant/aunt
assistance/assistants
ate/eight
ax/acts
bald/bawled
base/bass
be/bee
beach/beech
bear/bare
beat/beet
beau/bow
billed/build
bin/been
blew/blue
bored/board
brake/break
bruise/brews
but/butt
by/buy/bye
capital/capitol
cereal/serial
cheap/cheep
choir/quire
clause/claws
close/clothes
compliment/complement
council/counsel
course/coarse
creek/creak
deer/dear
die/dye
do/due/dew
doe/dough
fare/fair
feet/feat
fined/find
flower/flour

flue/flew
four/for/fore
fourth/forth
fur/fir
gate/gait
great/grate
grown/groan
guest/guessed
hair/hare
hale/hail
hay/hey
heal/heel/he'll
hear/here
heard/herd
high/hi
him/hymn
hoard/horde
horse/hoarse
I/eye
I'll/aisle/isle
in/inn
its/it's
kernel/colonel
knew/new/gnu
know/no
knows/nose
lane/lain
lay/lei
led/lead
lesson/lessen
made/maid
mail/male
main/mane
manner/manor
mantel/mantle
marry/merry
meat/meet
medal/meddle
might/mite
miner/minor
missed/mist
naval/navel
need/knead

night/knight
none/nun
not/knot
our/hour
packed/pact
pail/pale
pain/pane
pair/pear/pare
past/passed
patience/patients
pause/paws
peak/peek
pedal/peddle
piece/peace
plain/plane
pole/poll
pour/poor
pray/prey
presents/presence
principle/principal
rain/rein/reign
raise/rays
read/reed
real/reel
red/read
right/write/rite
road/rode
role/roll
rough/ruff
route/root
rows/rose
sail/sale
scene/seen
sea/see
sealing/ceiling
seas/sees/seize
seem/seam
sell/cell
sent/cent/scent

Homophones List (cont.)

shoot/chute
shown/shone
side/sighed
sight/site/cite
so/sew/sow
some/sum
sore/soar
soul/sole
stair/stare
stake/steak
stationary/stationery
stayed/staid
steal/steel
straight/strait
sun/son
surf/serf
sword/soared
tail/tale
taught/taut
tea/tee
tear/tier
their/there/they're
through/threw
tied/tide
time/thyme
toad/towed
toe/tow
two/to/too
urn/earn
vain/vane/vein
very/vary
waist/waste
way/weigh
we/wee
weak/week
weighed/wade
weight/wait
whale/wail
where/wear
whether/weather
while/wile
whole/hole
witch/which

won/one
wood/would
wrap/rap
wring/ring
you/ewe
you're/your/yore

Homophone Hunt

Directions: Highlight each homophone in the story. On a separate sheet of paper, list the words you highlighted with their homophones.

On the Rough Blue Sea

It was a gorgeous day for sailing on the big blue sea. The sun shone brightly and the wind blew hard. Our merry group settled in for a great trip. Suddenly, the sky became dark as night. Within seconds, rain began to pour down on us. Our boat was too weak to withstand the heavy downpour.

At first, all we could do was stare at each other. Steven ran down the stairs to close the portholes. Carmen hurried to the bin to find the life jackets. What a sight it was! The storm was at its highest peak. The waves rolled high, and the boat started tilting to the side. We tried loading weight on the other side. I shouted to Carmen, "We need to wear our life jackets!" As the waves rose higher, the wood of the boat began to creak. The rain continued to beat down on us. Two flashes of lightning lit the sky above. We held on for dear life and waited for the storm to pass.

Name _____ Date _____

Homophone Match

Rule
Homophones sound the same but have different meanings and spellings.

Directions: Write the number of the homophone next to its correct meaning.

1. write
2. feet
3. feat
4. mail
5. male
6. would
7. wood
8. taught
9. clause
10. minor
11. counsel
12. taut
13. claws
14. miner
15. council
16. air
17. heir
18. whole
19. hole
20. right

A. ____ opposite of *female*

B. ____ past tense of *will*

C. ____ from trees; used as building material and fuel

D. ____ great accomplishment

E. ____ the body parts you walk on

F. ____ material handled in the postal system

G. ____ to put words on paper

H. ____ tense

I. ____ person under legal age

J. ____ sharp, curved nails on an animal's foot

K. ____ correct; opposite of wrong

L. ____ group of words containing a subject and a verb

M. ____ past tense of *teach*

N. ____ colorless, odorless, gaseous mixture of nitrogen and oxygen

O. ____ one who inherits the estate of another

P. ____ all parts together

Q. ____ opening in something solid; a cavity or a pit

R. ____ group of people who have the power to govern or make laws

S. ____ person who works in a mine

T. ____ to offer an opinion or advice

Name _____ Date _____

Homophones in Letters

Directions: Cross out each incorrect homophone.
Write the correct homophone above it.

To: chris2@abc.net

From: david4@123.com

Subject: Last Weekend

(line 1)   Deer Chris,

(line 2)   I here that you were inn town last weekend. Eye am sorry that I mist

(line 3)   seeing you wile you were hear. The whether was sew bad that I was

(line 4)   knot able to make it out. I hope their mite be a weigh we can meat

(line 5)   if you are in town again next weak. Please say high too you're family

(line 6)   four me.

(line 7)   You're friend,

David

Write It Right

Directions: Write the correct homophones on the lines.

---

1. Bernie _____ to _____ his diet and eat fewer sweets.

(very/vary)   (kneads/needs)

---

2. Bella and Sam are going _____ _____ friend's house after

it stops _____.

(reining/raining/reigning)   (two/to/too)   (they're/there/their)

---

3. _____ will _____ the _____ shoes I bought on _____.

(wear/where)   (I/eye)   (new/knew)   (sale/sail)

---

4. The cowboy _____ his _____ over the dusty _____ until

the _____ set.

(son/sun)   (rode/road)   (plane/plain)   (hoarse/horse)

---

5. Maria lost her _____ when she couldn't _____ her gold _____ or

favorite _____ _____ .

(hare/hair)   (find/fined)   (beau/bow)   (wring/ring)   (patients/patience)

Homophone Quiz 1

Directions: Cross out each incorrect homophone. Write the correct homophone above it.

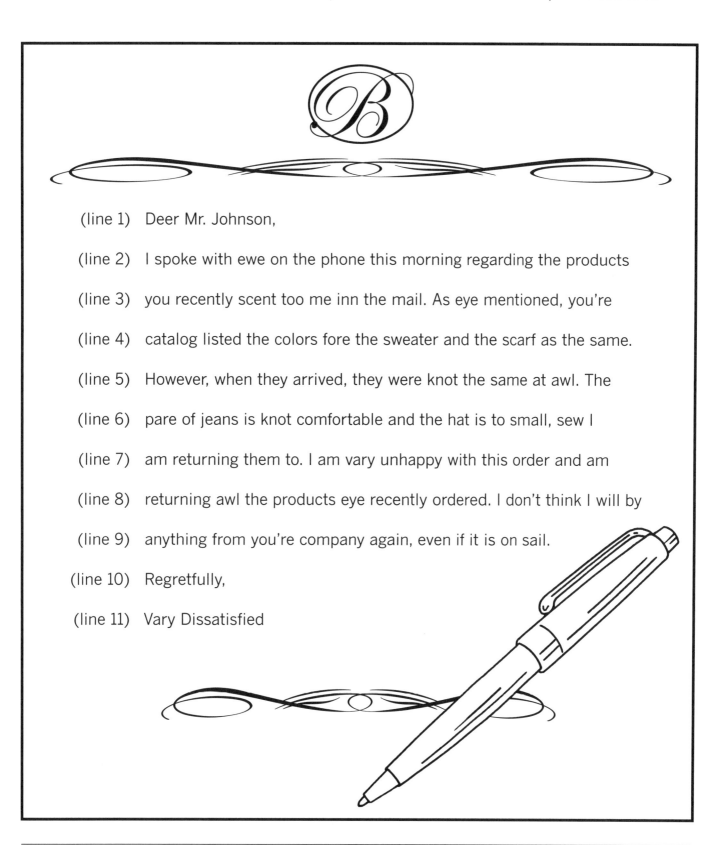

(line 1)   Deer Mr. Johnson,

(line 2)   I spoke with ewe on the phone this morning regarding the products

(line 3)   you recently scent too me inn the mail. As eye mentioned, you're

(line 4)   catalog listed the colors fore the sweater and the scarf as the same.

(line 5)   However, when they arrived, they were knot the same at awl. The

(line 6)   pare of jeans is knot comfortable and the hat is to small, sew I

(line 7)   am returning them to. I am vary unhappy with this order and am

(line 8)   returning awl the products eye recently ordered. I don't think I will by

(line 9)   anything from you're company again, even if it is on sail.

(line 10)   Regretfully,

(line 11)   Vary Dissatisfied

Name _____ Date _____

Homophone Quiz 2

Directions: Write the correct homophones on the lines.

---

1. Of _____ my stomach began _____ _____ during the seven

_____ meal at my uncle's _____ .

(course/coarse)   (two/to/too)   (grown/groan)   (course/coarse)   (manner/manor)

---

2. In the morning _____, I strolled between the _____ of _____ bushes

by _____ _____ building and noticed they were wet with _____ .

(hours/ours)   (rows/rose)   (rows/rose)   (hour/our)   (capitol/capital)   (do/due/dew)

---

3. _____ day the king lost his _____ , grabbed his _____ , and ran

through the early morning _____ _____ fight the _____ himself.

(One/Won) (patience/patients) (soared/sword) (missed/mist) (two/to/too) (nights/knights)

---

4. A fisherman must _____ _____ the water _____ fishing

_____ trout, even though _____ a _____ .

(weighed/wade)   (threw/through)   (wile/while)   (for/four/fore)   (its/it's)   (pain/pane)

---

5. _____ you _____ _____ pet _____ a _____ at bedtime if

it was really cute and had long ears?

(Wood/Would)   (read/reed)   (your/you're/yore)   (hair/hare)   (tail/tale)

CHAPTER 8

Assessment

The activities in this chapter assess what students have learned in the previous chapters. Each activity covers several different spelling rules and patterns. Use these activities as assessment tools or to determine where students might need additional work.

Pyramid Spelling Game

The "Pyramid Spelling Game" will engage and challenge students to think about words in general as well as how they are spelled. It is a great way for students to have fun while they collectively review and internalize the spelling rules they have learned.

Direct students to make pyramid-patterned lists of words in a set amount of time. Designate a letter of the alphabet that students must use at the beginning of their words. Give them two or three minutes to write words that start with the designated letter and whose spellings increase by one letter with each new word. Encourage students to think of spelling rules they have learned to help them recall words (e.g., adding suffixes, using contractions). You may wish to have students use word lists and charts from the previous activities as references. The student who writes the most correctly spelled words wins. Have the top three contenders write their pyramid of words on the board so all students can see and discuss the meanings of the words and check that the words are spelled correctly.

Pyramid Sample

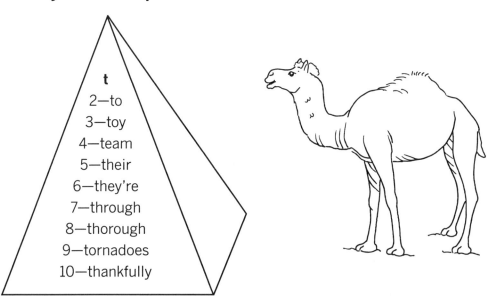

t
2—to
3—toy
4—team
5—their
6—they're
7—through
8—thorough
9—tornadoes
10—thankfully

Name the Rule

Directions: Proofread the following passage to find the spelling errors. Write the words correctly in the chart. Then find and circle correctly spelled words for each category.

A Better Tomorrow Starts Today

"As a educator, Iv'e always beleived that its important to recieve a good education if your going to obtain a excellent job," the teacher smiled at her students. "Lets talk about your posthigh school plans now."

A honor student dressed in kaki cloths replyed first. "I am planing to study science and later plan on becomeing a inventor."

"I would like to sea the writen requirements to be a pre-medical student. I no it will be challenging, but Id like to bee a doctor," ansered the girl siting next to hymn.

"I've always had the desire two be a paleontologist and study the pterosaurs. I want to speak publically about there disappearance," replied a third student.

The teacher noded with approval. These were students who new they're own minds and had already started to prepare for their future.

Spelling Rule	Incorrect	Correct
i Before *e*		
Using *a* and *an*		
Silent Letters		
Contractions		
Plural Nouns		
Prefixes		
Final *e* Rules		
Doubling Rules		
Change *y* to *i*		
al Rule		
ion/or Rule		
Homophones		

Name _____ Date _____

Is It Write?

Directions: Proofread to find the spelling errors. Write the words correctly in the chart.

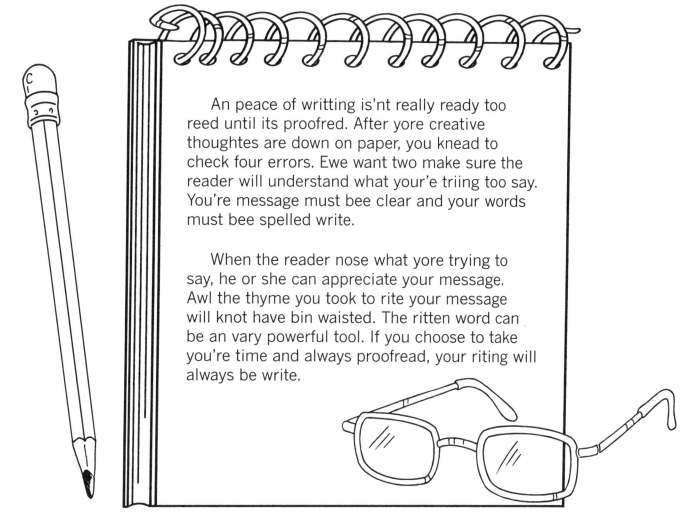

An peace of writting is'nt really ready too reed until its proofred. After yore creative thoughtes are down on paper, you knead to check four errors. Ewe want two make sure the reader will understand what your'e triing too say. You're message must bee clear and your words must bee spelled write.

When the reader nose what yore trying to say, he or she can appreciate your message. Awl the thyme you took to rite your message will knot have bin waisted. The ritten word can be an vary powerful tool. If you choose to take you're time and always proofread, your riting will always be write.

Spelling Rule	Incorrect	Correct
Using *a* and *an*		
Silent Letters		
Contractions		
Plural Nouns		
Final *e* Rules		
Ending *y* Rules		
Homophones		

Sum It Up: Spelling Review 1

Directions: Circle the incorrectly spelled words and write them in one column on a separate sheet of paper. Write the words correctly in a second column.

A Trip to the Zoo

Like many other boys, Stuart loved zoos. There were'nt any zoos in the small citys near his home. The best won in the hole world was in Sydney, less than a our away. He lived two far away from the buses to get to the zoo, so he took a train, always going into the coachs that had upstairs and downstairs seating.

As the train rattled along an route threw suburbs where knew immigrants from numerous countrys had settled, Stuart was'nt bored. He couldn't beleive some of the wierd sights he saw. He got off the train down by the wharves, looking for the ferries that took passengers to various beachs and sites around the harbor, including the zoo.

Once inside the zoo, Stuart headed straight four the Australian animals and observed them carefully. Kangaroos walked slowly on their tales with babys in they're pouches. Koalas lazily eight leafs or slept on branchs of gum trees. (There not a vary active speceis.) A pear of Tasmanian devils snarled at each other, baring and gnashing their tooths. In a oversized tank, platypuses swam busily and kicked their webbed foots. Nocturnal house residents like the flying foxs and kangaroo mice cautiously moved about in darkened habitats. (They are'nt friendly toward visiters unless you have pateince and wait quietly.)

Next, Stuart wandered among North American mammals that survived by grazing, like buffaloes, deers, mooses, caribou, and elks. Sometimes he wood pause by the oxen, but then he continued on toward the wolfs and bears. Stuart especially enjoyed watching the grizzly, a bear with course fur that often rows to its full hieght and shook the claws on it's pause.

When it was time to go, Stuart headed back to the main gate, past the gazebos overlooking a large pond where flamingoes, swans, and gooses stayed each night. As he heard the sad bleats of sheeps and calfs from the children's zoo, Stuart thought, "It willn't be long until Ia'm back." He reviewed his good day and smiled.

Sum It Up: Spelling Review 2

Directions: Circle the incorrectly spelled words and write them in one column on a separate sheet of paper. Write the words correctly in a second column.

Letter from a Friend

Dear Heather,

Hello from Hollywood! I'm amazed at how fast this year has past! It seems like only yesterday that I was studiing for my finales for last year. Now I'm basicly getting ready too do the same thing all over again. I'm faceing sum critically important assinments in these final weekes and am already panicing about how much writeing they will involve.

Of course, I have'nt stoped any of my extra activities. Artistically, my talents as a actor have growen. Specificly, I'm far better at learning and remembering my lines. I'am won of the few actors who has'nt blowen her lines in a performance or even in a ordinary rehearsal! My skills at mimicking others are steadyly improving. One directer is hopful that next year I will have starring rolls in at least haf of hour major productions.

With the increasingly warmer whether, I am more athleticly inclined and am spending much more leisure time outdoors. That also gives me an excuse for sliping away to go picnicing. Last weekend, one of my nieghbors maid some incredibly garlicy shrimps. They were fantastically delicious!

Realisticly, I know aisle get threw it all and that I was dramaticly exaggerating when I said how hopeless things appeared. My professers told me that I have shown a exceptional amount of growth this year. I expect that I'll be recieving grades that my parents will find drastically better than those from last year. Still, I can't weight until the begining of the holidayes!

Oops! There's less than a hour until my next class, and my work is'nt finished yet. I'd better get going. Maybe this year we'll figure out an weigh to get together, my freind. Stay well and rite soon.

Love,

Maya

Answer Key

PAGE 9
1. reindeer
2. freight
3. veins
4. niece
5. seize
6. weird
7. eighty
8. friend
9. believe
10. neighbor
11. no
12. yes
13. yes
14. no
15. yes
16. no
17. yes
18. yes
19. yes
20. yes
21. no
22. no
23 yes
24. yes
25. yes
26. no
27. no
28. yes
29. yes
30. no

PAGE 10
receive	niece	believed
patient	relieved	shrieks
deceiving	piece	chief
freight	reign	reindeer
friend	sleigh	reviewed
weighed	eighty	reins
neighbor		

1. niece
2. reins
3. reindeer
4. believed
5. eighty
6. sleigh
7. chief
8. neighbor (friend)
9. reign
10. Shrieks
11. freight
12. receive
13. piece
14. patient
15. deceiving
16. weighed
17. relieved
18. reviewed
19. friend (neighbor)

PAGE 11
1. neighbor's
2. believe
3. veins
4. either
5. height
6. niece
7. deceiving
8. reviewed
9. species
10. patience
11. neigh
12. beige
13. field
14. veil
15. leisure
16. piece
17. tie
18. their
19. thief
20. pier
21. grief
22. pie

PAGE 12
1. eighteen
2. reindeer
3. quiet
4. patient
5. their
6. freight
7. sleigh
8. neither
9. chief
10. weird
11. friendly
12. reviewed
13. weighed
14. height
15. eighty
16. species
17. reigned
18. either
19. leisure
20. believe
21. seize
22. reins
23. shrieks
24. neighborhood
25. piece
26. receive
27. veil
28. deceive
29. veins
30. niece

PAGE 15
1. a/a
2. a/an
3. an/an
4. an/a
5. an/a
6. a/an
7. a/an
8. a/an
9. an/a
10. a/an
11. an/a
12. a/an
13. a/a
14. a/an
15. an/an
16. an/a
17. a/an
18. a/an
19. a/a
20. an/a

PAGE 16
1. yes
2. yes
3. no
4. no
5. yes
6. no
7. yes
8. no
9. yes
10. no
11. no
12. no
13. yes
14. yes
15. yes
16. no
17. yes
18. no
19. no
20. yes

PAGE 17
A
hungry student	woman
giant elephant	blurry X ray
professor	neighbor
long hour	huge umbrella
situation	humorous situation
university	hybrid automobilefaint
SOS signal	story
game	hand
soft hand	disappointing F grade

AN
energetic woman	endangered eagle
elephant	X ray
intelligent professor	honest neighbor
hour	umbrella
old university	automobile
SOS signal	interesting story
unbelievable game	F grade

PAGE 18
H
1. a
2. a
3. an
4. an
5. a
6. a
7. a
8. a
9. a
10. a
11. a
12. a
13. a
14. an
U
1. an
2. a
3. an
4. a
5. an
6. a
7. an
8. a
9. a
10. a
11. a
12. an
13. an
14. an

PAGE 19
1. an
2. a
3. an
4. an
5. a
6. an
7. a
8. a
9. a
10. an
11. a
12. an
13. a
14. a
15. a
16. an
17. an
18. a
19. a
20. an
21. a
22. an
23. A
24. an
25. a
26. an
27. an
28. A
29. an
30. an
31. an
32. a
33. a
34. a
35. a

PAGE 20
1. an
2. a
3. a
4. an
5. a
6. an
7. a
8. A
9. a
10. an
11. an
12. an
13. a
14. a
15. An
16. an
17. an
18. a
19. an
20. a
21. an
22. an
23. a
24. An
25. an
26. a
27. an
28. an
29. a
30. an

31. a
32. an
33. an
34. an
35. a
36. an

PAGE 21
1. an/a/an
2. a/an/an
3. a/an/an
4. a/an/a
5. an/a/an
6. an/a/a
7. a/an/a
8. an/a/an
9. an/a/an
10. a/a/a
11. an/a/a
12. a/an/a

PAGES 26–30
Answers will vary.

PAGE 31
1. climb
2. comb
3. crumbs
4. debt
5. doubt
6. dumbfounded
7. lamb
8. limb
9. plumber
10. thumb
11. dumbfounded
12. climb
13. limb
14. debt
15. plumber
16. thumb
17. lamb
18. crumbs
19. comb
20. doubt

PAGE 32
1. gnu, knew, new
2. gnome
3. gnarl
4. gnu
5. resign
6. gnaw
7. gnat
8. herb, hour, honest, honesty, honor
9. hurrah, rhyme, Thomas
10. hour (our)
11.–12. Answers will vary.

PAGE 33
The word *now* is pronounced differently.
The word *know* should be circled.
The following words should be underlined:
knight	know	knob
knew	knot	knit

1.–10. Answers will vary.

PAGE 34
1. could
2. salmon
3. half
4. folks
5. calf
6. calm
7. talk
8. should
9. palm
10. would
11. salve
12. yolk

How much <u>wood</u> <u>would</u> a woodchuck chuck,
if a woodchuck <u>could</u> chuck <u>wood</u>?
A woodchuck <u>would</u> chuck as much <u>wood</u>
as a woodchuck <u>could</u> chuck,
if a woodchuck <u>could</u> chuck <u>wood</u>.

PAGE 35
1. pteridology
2. psychic
3. pneumonia
4. pteranodon

978-1-4129-5826-4

Answer Key

PAGE 35 (CONT.)
5. psychology
6. ptarmigan
7. pneumograph
8. pterosaur
9. pseudonym
10. psychedelic
11. pterodactyl
12. psoriasis

PAGE 36
1. bristle 2 bris-tle
2. bustle 2 bus-tle
3. castle 2 cas-tle
4. gristle 2 gris-tle
5. hustle 2 hus-tle
6. rustle 2 rus-tle
7. thistle 2 this-tle
8. whistle 2 whis-tle
9. fasten 2 fas-ten
10. glisten 2 glis-ten
11. hasten 2 has-ten
12. listen 2 lis-ten
13. moisten 2 mois-ten
14. The silent *t* always belongs to the second syllable.

PAGE 37
1. wristwatch 2. wriggle 3. wring
4. wrap 5. wreckage 6. wreath
7. wrong 8. wretch 9. wrestler
10. wrinkle 11. wren 12. wrist
13. wrinkle 14. write 15. sword
16. wretch 17. wrap 18. wring
19. wrong 20. wristwatch

PAGE 38
b—doubted, numb, lambs, debt, Climb
g—assignment, gnome, sign
h—honest, hours, Thomas, honor
k—knight, knew, knock, kneeled, known
l—talkative, could, should, half, calf, calves, calm, palm, would
p— pterodactyl, pterosaur's
t—listen, rustle, hastened, castle, glistened
w—wrong, wreaked, sword, Wrapped

PAGE 42
Check that students followed directions.

PAGE 43
Check that students followed directions.

PAGE 45
1. won't 2. He's 3. we're
4. I'm 5. won't 6. They're
7. he'll 8. wouldn't 9. should've
10. Let's 11. a 12. ha
13. a 14. i or ha 15. a
16. o 17. ill 18. o
19. a 20. u

PAGE 46
1. didn't 2. I'm 3. no
4. didn't 5. hasn't 6. won't
7. won't 8. won't 9. He'll
10. no 11. What's 12. You've
13. no 14. I'll 15. You'll
16. no 17. that's

PAGE 47
Isn't = is not
I'll = I will
That's = that is
It's = it is
can't = can not
it's = it is
Who's = who is
Wouldn't = would not
I'm = I am
We're = we are
aren't = are not
we'll = we will
You're = you are
You'll = you will
What's = what is
doesn't = does not
You've = you have
There's = there is
won't = will not
couldn't = could not
They'll = they will
haven't = have not
we'd = we would

PAGE 48
1. who's 2. won't
3. we'll 4. what's
5. let's 6. don't
7. he'd 8. she's
9. who'd 10. how's
11. a 12. ha or woul
13. o 14. a
15. ha 16. o
17. a 18. a
19. i or ha 20. ha

The Beautiful Little Bee
line 1—don't
line 2—It's
line 3—I'm, we're, there's
line 4—We'll
line 5—you're or aren't, I'll
line 6—wouldn't, won't
line 7—none

PAGE 52
1. es/witches 2. s/coats
3. es/glasses 4. s/tables
5. es/speeches 6. es/foxes
7. s/flags 8. es/princesses
9. es/wishes 10. es/sphinxes
11. es/benches 12. s/steaks
13. es/dishes 14. es/faxes
15. no, valleys 16. yes, babies
17. no, boys 18. yes, spies
19. yes, countries 20. no, keys
21. no, toys 22. yes, berries
23. no, freeways 24. yes, cities
25. yes, skies 26. no, trays
27. yes, stories 28. yes, dairies

PAGE 53
1. elk 2. geese
3. deer 4. feet
5. mice 6. women
7. moose 8. caribou
9. children 10. men
11. shrimp 12. sheep

13. oxen 14. teeth
15. swine

PAGE 54
1. children 2. buses 3. sheep
4. leaders 5. women 6. schools
7. monkeys 8. beliefs 9. speeches
10. events 11. babies 12. cities
13. freeways 14. students 15. men
16. wives 17. boys 18. girls
19. promises 20. wishes 21. echoes
22. Parents 23. bays 24. buses
25. boxes 26. loaves 27. batches
28. sandwiches 29. containers
30. strawberries 31. hatches 32. Drivers
33. watches 34. keys 35. switches
36. coaches 37. moms 38. feet
39. eyelashes 40. tears 41. eyes
42. kisses 43. ones 44. lives
45. travelers 46. windows 47. hills
48. valleys 49. deer 50. foxes
51. calves 52. glasses 53. smells
54. mice 55. butterflies
56. messes 57. wipers 58. bodies
59. princes 60. princesses
61. days 62. places
63. journeys 64. youngsters

PAGE 55
1. wishes, children, boys
2. monkeys, sheep, wolves
3. geese, toys, bushes
4. lives, days, moose
5. turkeys, men, hooves
6. dishes, species, keys
7. elves, feet, countries
8. lunches, ladies, deer
9. branches, mice, balloons
10. teeth, ladders, leaves
11. spiders, oxen, witches
12. women, tigers, bunches
13. eyes, clouds, wives
14. rooms, sheep, switches
15. moose, lights, boxes
16. books, teeth, loaves
17. foxes, deer, stars
18. recesses, hotels, women
19. oxen, businesses, calves
20. children, bicycles, taxes

PAGE 56
Answers will vary.

PAGE 61
1. illogical — not logical
2. overeating — eating too much
3. unfriendly — not friendly
4. misunderstanding — wrong understanding
5. unfortunately — not fortunately
6. unhappy — not happy
7. underestimated — estimated too little
8. displeasure — the opposite of *pleasure*
9. unflustered — not flustered
10. superhero — above a hero
11. recovered — to take back again
12. immature — not mature
13. overindulging — indulging too much

Answer Key

PAGE 62
1. unprotected
2. regain
3. unproven
4. dislike
5. immoral
6. irregular
7. illegal
8. transport
9. trans-Atlantic
10. unfriendly
11. interact
12. misstate
13. subway
14. midnight
15. superhero
16. overeat
17. overprotective
18. semicircle
19. underestimate
20. unequal
21. misspell
22. disapprove
23. rewrite
24. overpay
25. inhuman
26. preplan
27. nonsense
28. impossible
29. transcontinental
30. irrational

PAGE 63
1. unhappy
2. interstate
3. impolite
4. forecast
5. irrevocable
6. irrefutable
7. miscommunicate
8. unsatisfied
9. underestimate
10. midsummer
11. preview
12. pre-Columbian
13. misspeak
14. irrecoverable
15. impatient
16. improper
17. redo
18. restart
19. misplace
20. forethought

PAGE 66
Answers will vary.

PAGE 67
1. hiked
2. riding
3. baking
4. serving
5. facing
6. traced
7. dining
8. writing
9. using
10. faked
11. no
12. no
13. yes
14. yes
15. no
16. no
17. yes
18. yes
19. no
20. no
21. making
22. careless
23. bees
24. named
25. useful
26. widest
27. livable
28. dines
29. nameless
30. hopeful

PAGE 68
1. paper—2
2. wait—1
3. book—1
4. listen—2
5. tip—1
6. umbrella—3
7. think—1
8. computer—3
9. treasure—2
10. sip—1
11. stop—CVC
12. skip—CVC
13. look—VVC
14. jump—VCC
15. dig—CVC
16. play—CVC
17. start—VCC
18. smile—VCV
19. eat—VVC
20. stir—CVC
21. trapped
22. playful
23. stopping
24. skipped
25. joyful
26. thinker
27. napping
28. sitting
29. sinking
30. skipper

PAGE 69
1. studying
2. hurried
3. shyness
4. sturdiness
5. busily
6. crier
7. trying
8. worrying
9. emptying
10. copied
11. betrays
12. playing
13. playful
14. boyish
15. staying
16. buying
17. sprayed
18. laying
19. joyful
20. conveys
21. shining
22. happiness
23. stopped
24. saying
25. wanted
26. writing
27. skipped
28. joyful
29. biggest
30. thinking
31. shortest
32. hoped

PAGE 70
1. picnicking
2. colicky
3. garlicky
4. gimmicky
5. panicking
6. mimicking
7. trafficked
8. panicked
9. no
10. yes
11. no
12. yes
13. no
14. yes
15. yes
16. no
17. yes
18. no
19. yes
20. yes

PAGE 71
1. blown
2. grown
3. known
4. flown
5. shown
6. sown
7. mown
8. thrown
9. no
10. no
11. no
12. yes
13. no
14. yes
15. yes
16. grown—When a word ends with w, add the suffix -en and drop the e.
17. picnicker—When words end with c, add k before suffixes that begin with e, i, or y.
18. crying—Change y to i when a word ends in a consonant and y, and the suffix is anything but -ing.
19. parties—Change y to i when a word ends in a consonant and y, and the suffix is anything but -ing.
20. blurred—Double the last consonant when a one-syllable word ends with CVC and the suffix begins with a V (vowel).
21. baking—Drop the final e when the suffix begins with a vowel.

PAGE 72
1. automatically
2. scientifically
3. logically
4. enthusiastically
5. basically
6. frantically
7. musically
8. magically
9. yes
10. no
11. yes
12. no
13. yes
14. yes
15. no
16.–17. Answers will vary.

PAGE 73
1. instruction — instructor
2. no — designer
3. projection — projector
4. education — educator
5. no — planter
6. injection — injector
7. invention — inventor
8. action — actor
9. direction — director
10. no — speaker
11. inspection — inspector
12. no — photographer
13. no — helper
14. celebration — celebrator
15. no — singer

PAGE 74
Correctly spelled or words form the letter S. The following words should be circled: dictator, projector, injector, detector, celebrator, actor, elector, imitator, collector, compressor, inspector, evaluator, visor, realtor, motivator, contractor, director, instructor, professor, tractor, transgressor, confessor

PAGE 75
1. A, hopeful
2. D, panicked
3. G, inspector
4. E, blown
5. B, jogging
6. F, magically
7. A, writing
8. B, skipping
9. C, hurried
10. G, actor

PAGE 81
It was a gorgeous day for sailing on the big blue sea. The sun shone brightly and the wind blew hard. Our merry group settled in for a great trip. Suddenly, the sky became dark as night. Within seconds, rain began to pour down on us. Our boat was too weak to withstand the heavy downpour. At first, all we could do was stare at each other. Steven ran down the stairs to close the portholes. Carmen hurried to the bin to find the life jackets. What a sight it was! The storm was at its highest peak. The waves rolled high, and the boat started tilting to the side. We tried loading weight on the other side. I shouted to Carmen, "We need to wear our life jackets!" As the waves rose higher, the wood of the boat began to creak. The rain continued to beat down on us. Two flashes of lightning lit the sky above. We held on for dear life and waited for the storm to pass.
blue/blew
sea/see
sun/son
shone/shown

978-1-4129-5826-4

Answer Key

PAGE 81 (CONT.)

blew/blue
Our/hour
merry/marry
in/inn
for/four/fore
great/grate
night/knight
rain/reign/rein
to/two/too
pour/poor/pore
Our/hour
too/two/to
weak/week
to/two/too
all/awl
we/wee
do/due
stare/stair
stairs/stares
to/two/too
close/clothes
to/two/too
bin/been
to, two, too
find/fined
sight/site/cite
its/it's
peak/peek
high/hi
to/two/too
side/sighed
We/wee
weight/wait
side/sighed
I/eye
to/two/too
We/wee
need/knead
to/two/too
where/wear/ware
our/hour
rose/rows
wood/would
to/two/too
creak/creek
rain/reign/rein
to/two/too
beat/beet
Two/to/too
We/wee
for/four/fore
dear/deer
waited/weighted
for/four/fore
to/two/too

PAGE 82

A.	5	**B.**	6
C.	7	**D.**	3
E.	2	**F.**	4
G.	1	**H.**	12
I.	10	**J.**	13
K.	20	**L.**	9
M.	8	**N.**	16
O.	17	**P.**	18
Q.	19	**R.**	15

S.	14	**T.**	11

PAGE 83

line 1—Dear
line 2—hear, in, I, missed
line 3—while, here, weather, so
line 4—not, there, might, way, meet
line 5—week, hi, to, your
line 6—for
line 7—Your

PAGE 84

1. needs, vary
2. to, their, raining
3. I, wear, new, sale
4. rode, horse, plain, sun
5. patience, find, ring, hair, bow

PAGE 85

line 1—Dear
line 2—you
line 3—sent, to, in, I, your
line 4—for
line 5—not, all
line 6—pair, not, too, so
line 7—too, very
line 8—all, I, buy
line 9—your, sale
line 10—none
line 11—Very

PAGE 86

1. course, to, groan, course, manor
2. hours, rows, rose, our, capitol, dew
3. One, patience, sword, mist, to, knights
4. wade, through, while, for, it's, pain
5. Would, read, your, hare, tale

PAGE 88

The words from the story are listed according to their spelling category. The words with errors are underlined.
i-before-*e* Rule—believed, receive, replied, their
Using *a* and *an*—an educator, a good education, an excellent job, An honor student, an inventor, a pre-medical student, a doctor, a paleontologist, a third student
Silent Letters—talk, honor, khaki, written, answered, pterosaurs
Contractions— I've, it's, you're, Let's, I'd
Plural Nouns—students, plans, clothes, requirements, pterosaurs, students, minds
Prefixes—pre-medical, post-high school
Final *e* Rules—believed, smiled, becoming, challenging
Doubling Rules—planning, written, sitting, nodded
Ending *y* Rules—replied
al Rule—publicly (exception)
ion/or Rule—educator, inventor
Homophones—it's, to, you're, your, in, clothes, I, would, see, be, know, but, be, him, to, their, knew, their, to, for, their

PAGE 89

The words from the story are listed according to their spelling category.
Using *a* and *an*—A piece of writing, a very powerful tool
Silent Letters—writing, write, written, writing
Contractions—isn't, it's, you're
Plural Nouns—thoughts
Final *e* Rules—writing, writing
Ending *y* Rules—trying
Homophones—piece, to, read, it's, proofread, your, need, for, You, to, you're, to, Your, be, be, right, knows, you're, to, your, All, time, write, not, been, wasted, very, your, right

PAGE 90

Paragraph 1—weren't, cities, one, whole, an, hour, too, coaches
Paragraph 2—a route, through, new, countries, wasn't, believe, weird, beaches
Paragraph 3—for, tails, babies, their, ate, leaves, branches, They're, very, species, pair, teeth, an oversized, feet, foxes, aren't, visitors, patience
Paragraph 4—deer, moose, elk, would, wolves, coarse, rose, height, its, paws
Paragraph 5—geese, sheep, calves, won't, I'm

PAGE 91

Paragraph 1—passed, studying, finals, basically, to, facing, some, assignments, weeks, panicking, writing
Paragraph 2—haven't, stopped, an actor, grown, Specifically, I'm, one, hasn't, blown, an ordinary, steadily, director, hopeful, roles, half, our
Paragraph 3—weather, athletically, slipping, picnicking, neighbors, made, garlicky, shrimp
Paragraph 4—Realistically, I'll, through, dramatically, professors, an exceptional, receiving, wait, beginning, holidays
Paragraph 5—an hour, isn't, a, way, friend, write

References

American heritage college dictionary (4th ed.). (2004). Boston, MA: Houghton Mifflin.

Blevins, W. (1998). *Phonics from A to Z: A practical guide.* New York, NY: Scholastic.

Dixon, R., & Engelmann, S. (2001). *Spelling through morphographs.* Columbus, OH: SRA/McGraw-Hill.

Ehri, L. C. (1991). Learning to read and spell words. In L. Rieben & C. A. Perfetti (Eds.), *Learning to read: Basic research and its implications* (pp. 57–73). Hillsdale, NJ: Lawrence Erlbaum.

Gibaldi, J. (2003). *MLA handbook for writers of research papers.* New York, NY: The Modern Language Association of America.

Graham, S., & Miller, L. (1979). Spelling research and practice: A unified approach. *Focus on Exceptional Children, 12*(2), 75–91.

Greene, J. F. (2005). *Language! The comprehensive literacy curriculum.* Longmont, CO: Sopris West.

McEwan, E. K. (2002). *Teach them all to read: Catching the kids who fall through the cracks.* Thousand Oaks, CA: Corwin Press.

Moats, L. C. (2003). *LETRS: Language essentials for teachers of reading and spelling.* Longmont, CO: Sopris West.

More Words. (n.d.). *More words.* Retrieved March 17, 2007, from http://www.morewords.com.

Nater, S., & Gallimore, R. (2006). *You haven't taught until they have learned: John Wooden's teaching principles and practices.* Morgantown, WV: Fitness Information Technology.

Personke, C., & Yee, A. (1971). *Comprehensive spelling instruction: Theory, research, and application.* Scranton, PA: Intext Educational Publishers.

Scholastic dictionary of synonyms, antonyms, and homonyms. (2001). New York, NY: Scholastic Reference.

Word Files. (n.d.). *Uses and misuses of English words.* Retrieved March 10, 2006, from http://www.wordfiles.info/.

Word Navigator. (n.d.). *List all words ending with ow.* Retrieved March 16, 2006, from http://wordnavigator.com/ends-with/ow/.